Personality Development

Personality Development
TRANSFORM YOURSELF

Rajiv K Mishra

RUPA

Copyright © Rajiv K Mishra 2004

First Published 2004
Seventeenth Impression 2012

Published by
Rupa Publications India Pvt. Ltd.
7/16, Ansari Road, Daryaganj,
New Delhi 110 002

Sales Centres:
Allahabad Bengaluru Chennai
Hyderabad Jaipur Kathmandu
Kolkata Mumbai

All rights reserved.
No part of this publication may be reproduced, stored in a retrieval system, or transmitted, in any form or by any means, electronic, mechanical, photocopying, recording or otherwise, without the prior permission of the publishers.

Typeset in 11 pts. Classical Garamond by
Mindways Design
1410 Chiranjiv Tower
43 Nehru Place
New Delhi 110 019

Printed in India by
Saurabh Printers Pvt. Ltd.
A-16, Sector-IV
Noida-201 301

The author dedicates this book to his mother, late Sushila. She was a lady of extraordinary will-power. She had great strength to fight all odds and was a true believer in a person's capability and potential to transform into a great personality. The author feels privileged to have had his childhood nurtured under the sensitive and able guidance of his mother.

Contents

Introduction	ix
1. Know your Personality	1
Section I: Behavioural Traits	27
2. Communication Skills	29
3. Sharpen your Communication Skills	41
4. Motivation and Self-Motivation	89
5. Leadership Qualities and Ways to Influence Others	101
6. Influence of Friends on your Personality	116
7. Etiquette and Mannerism	119
8. Sense of Humour	133
9. Interpersonal Relationships	139
10. Enhance your Effectiveness	175
11. Time Management—Organise Yourself	185
12. Manage the Complexes	190
Section II: Positive Attitude	203
13. Positive Attitude Towards Life	205

14. Dare to Think Big and Win 217

Section III: Character Traits 221

15. Ethics & Values 223

Section IV: Action Plan 231

16. Career Planning 233
17. How to Write an Impressive Résumé 237
18. Power Dressing–An investment 244
19. Develop a Hobby 249
20. Importance of Fitness and Yoga 254
21. Personality of the New Millennium 260
22. Pray to God for your Well-Being 269
    References 273

Introduction

A man is identified by his personality. It is the public image of what a person is, how he is perceived in society. We at times mistake it for physical appearance, dress-sense and looks. It is the totality of a person and not merely the external looks, but character, behavioural traits and attitude towards life. The million-dollar question is, "Can a person transform his personality?" The answer is an emphatic YES!

The behavioural scientists have proved that a person with low self-esteem, morale and low effectiveness can be transformed into a successful personality. In the history of mankind we have numerous examples to corroborate what the behavioural scientists have put forward.

This book acts as a manual for young students who are ready to plunge into the highly competitive world. A practical, direct-action, personality enhancement guideline, it is written with the sole intention of acquainting young readers with some of the harsh realities and not-so-sweet facts of life, which are generally learnt the hard way. The author has tried to assimilate the concepts and cases of personality enhancement in a lucid way to impress the mind of the reader.

This book is written to suggest personality enhancement techniques and to give examples which demonstrate that you can be a better personality, can have better peace of mind, improved health and can generate the energy to make yourself successful. Like many other persons who have learnt and applied the simple procedures to transform themselves into a better personality, you too can achieve the winning touch.

We are at times bogged down by small and petty problems in our life that irritate us. We cannot ignore the hardship and tragedies of life, but if they dominate our personality, it is bound to have negative effects. This book is an attempt to find out how to cast them out from our mind. If we refuse to become mentally submissive to them, we can channel our thoughts, energy and deeds in a positive direction. Our thoughts and actions must always reflect a positive attitude towards life.

The behavioural traits—communication skills, interpersonal relationships, the positive influence of relationships—are all important to transform a person into an effective human being. We are all part of a large society, nation and a global community. A person cannot expect to perform well if he cannot develop a positive working relationship with his team members. The best of intentions are defeated if not communicated well.

This book has been written to assimilate all the aspects of personality development with the need of Graduation level students in mind. The author will be grateful to all readers for their valuable suggestions and feedback to improve the book in the next edition.

Wish you a pleasant and charming personality,

Kolkata   Rajiv K Mishra

1

Know Your Personality

The Oxford dictionary defines 'personality traits' as 'a person's distinctive character'. The personality of an individual accompanies him anywhere and everywhere he goes and exhibits itself in whatever he does. Most people mistake physical attributes of an individual as his/her personality. They talk about a marvellous personality when they may just be referring to an individual's stature, fair complexion or chiselled features.

Well, if you thought that personality has anything to do with height, good looks, complexion or the physique of a person, it is time you re-think what you think you know. Any physical shortcomings can hardly influence your personality. A person of repute is identified because of his personality traits such as superior character and behaviour, and not by other mundane and frivolous considerations.

2 Personality Development

As per modern management concepts, "Personality is the BRAND IMAGE of an individual." It is made up of three broad aspects, namely:

1. Character (few behavioural authors have a different opinion that character has little to do with personality, but in this book we shall consider it as its foundation)
2. Behavioural traits
3. Attitude

Personality development is the improvement of behavioural traits such as communication skills, interpersonal relationships, attitude towards life and restoring our ethics. Character is the prerequisite to achieving a better individual personality. There are several behavioural scientists who argue that improving behavioural traits in a short-cut course of fifteen days to develop personality can effectively influence others and help win the race. But we must never forget that excellent behavioural traits such as communication skills, interpersonal relationships, higher order of motivational levels and excellent leadership qualities also fail miserably at the time of crisis if not based on solid character foundation.

Behaviour is just the showcase of the larger inventory inside a person, i.e. character. If personality is developed on the solid base of values and ethics, it will last forever. Fake smiles and mannerisms are short-lived and do not help in improving one's personality.

Know your Personality

Personality Development

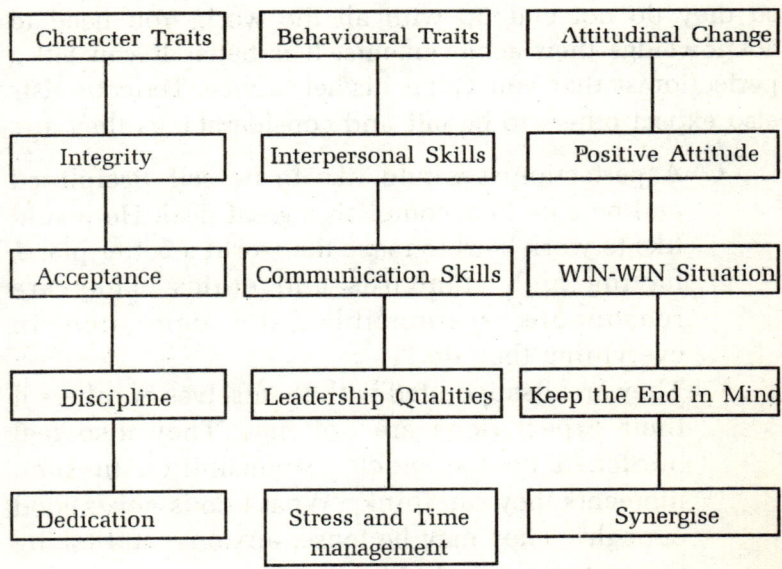

Types of Personality

Well-known behavioural scientists and psychologists have identified many types of personalities. We shall concentrate on the nine types of personalities. These are– Perfectionists, Helpers, Romantics, Achievers, Asserters, Questioners, Adventurers, Observers and Peacemakers. They have their own unique personality traits that are briefly analysed below.

1. *The Perfectionist*

Perfectionists are realistic, conscientious and principled. They strive to live up to their high ideals. They can be got along well with if you take your share of the responsibilities so they do not end up with all the work. You need to acknowledge their achievements. It is better if you tell a perfectionist that you value his/her advice. Perfectionists also expect others to be fair and considerate, as they are.

- A perfectionist would like to be self-disciplined and be able to accomplish a great deal. He would like to work hard to make the world a better place, having high standards and ethics. They are reasonable, responsible, and dedicated in everything they do.
- They are disappointed with themselves or others if their expectations are not met. They also feel burdened by too much responsibility. In such moments they can think, "What I do is never good enough". They may be tense, anxious, and taking things too seriously.

Example: The great Indian software business leader Narayan Murthy falls in the category of a perfectionist. Another name that fits the bill is pole-vault world record holder, Sergei Bubka of Ukraine, who always strived to better his own record.

2. *The Helper*

Helpers are warm, concerned, nurturing, and sensitive to other people's needs. They can be got along well with if you tell them that you appreciate them. They would expect you to share fun times with them. They would like you to take interest in their problems, though they will probably try to focus on yours. They want you to know that they are important and special to you.

- A helper likes to be able to relate easily to people and make friends, know what people need and be able to make their lives better. They are generous, caring and warm. They are sensitive to and perceptive about others' feelings. They are fun-loving and generally possess a good sense of humour.
- A helper faces a problem when he is not able to say no. They have low self-esteem and are drained due to overdoing things for others. They cannot do things they really like to do for themselves for fear of being selfish.

Example: Mother Teresa is one such personality who was sensitive not only to the needs of few people around, but for the millions of poor in the country.

3. *The Achiever*

Achievers are energetic, optimistic, self-assured, and goal-oriented.

- An achiever gets along well with his co-workers. He welcomes honest, but not unduly critical or judgmental, feedback. He expects you to keep his environment harmonious and peaceful. You cannot

burden him with negative emotions. He likes being optimistic, friendly and upbeat, and likes to provide well for his family. He is happy if he stays informed, knowing what's going on.
- Achievers face problems when they have to put up with inefficiency and incompetence. They are gripped with the fear of failure or of not being seen as successful. They keep on struggling to hang on to their success.

Example: Sachin Tendulkar, the greatest batsman, and Kapil Dev, the greatest all-rounder, fall in the category of achievers—always full of energy to achieve something big.

4. *The Romantic*

Romantics have sensitive feelings and are warm and perceptive.

- A romantic would like to get plenty of compliments. They mean a lot to them. He expects you to be a supportive friend or partner. If you care for him you respect him for his special gifts of intuition and vision. He would like to, establish warm connections with people, admire what is noble, truthful, and beautiful in life; he would like to be creative, intuitive, and have a sense of humour. He is unique and is seen as unique by others.
- A romantic faces a problem when he is experiencing dark moods of emptiness and despair, feelings of self-hatred and shame; believing he

does not deserve to be loved, feeling hurt or attacked when someone misunderstands him, fearing being abandoned, longing for what he does not have.

Example: The great Indian painter M.F. Hussain falls in the type of romantic personality. He has a sensitive heart and romantic personality for his creativity.

5. *The Observer*

Observers have a need for knowledge and are introverted, curious, analytical, and insightful.

- An observer likes to be independent, not clingy. He prefers to speak in a straightforward and brief manner. He desires and needs time alone to process his feelings and thoughts and may doubt your sincerity if you intensely welcome him. He dislikes intrusions on his privacy. He remains calm in a crisis.
- An observer faces a problem when he/she is not sure of the situation and is unable to understand the relation between cause and effect. He gets disturbed if his integrity is doubted.

Example: The great economist and Nobel laureate Amartya Sen is one such observer personality, who is curious, analytical and insightful.

6. *The Questioner*

Questioners are responsible and trustworthy. They value loyalty to family, friends, groups and causes. Their personalities range broadly, from reserved and timid to outspoken.

- A questioner likes to be direct and clear. He likes others to listen to him carefully. You are required to reassure him that 'everything is ok between us' and not judge him for his anxiety. He is committed and faithful to family and friends, responsible and hardworking, compassionate towards others, direct and assertive.
- A questioner faces a problem when under constant push and pull, involved in trying to make up his/her mind. He fears failure, having little confidence in his own ability. He tends to be too critical of himself when he has not lived up to his own expectations.

Example: The outspoken Bollywood actress and former Rajya Sabha member, Shabana Azmi, may fall in the category of a questioner. She can raise relevant questions in all platforms.

7. *The Adventurer*

Adventurers are energetic, lively, and optimistic. They want to contribute to the world.

- An adventurer likes to get companionship, affection and freedom. He likes engaging you in stimulating conversation and laughter, and expects you to appreciate his grand visions and listen to his stories. He is optimistic and does not let life's troubles get him down. He is spontaneous and free-spirited.

- An adventurer faces a problem when he does not have enough time to do all the things he wants to and is unable to complete the things he starts.

Example: The energetic NRI businessman, Vijay Mallaya, may be categorised in the adventurer type for trying something new that was not done by any Indian earlier.

8. *The Asserter*

Asserters are direct, self-reliant, self-confident and protective.

- An asserter likes to stand up for you and is confident, strong and direct. He is vulnerable and shares his feelings and at the same time acknowledges your tender, vulnerable side. He likes to get space to be alone. He is curious to hear about his own contributions, but do not flatter him. He likes being independent and self-reliant, able to take charge and meet challenges head on. He is courageous, straightforward, honest, supporting, empowering and protective of those close to him.
- An asserter faces a problem when he is being restless and impatient with others' incompetence, receiving no appreciation for good work done for others.

Example: The former Chief Election Commissioner, T.N. Seshan, the straightforward bold officer, is the best Indian example of an asserter.

9. *The Peacemaker*

Peacemakers are receptive, good-natured and supportive. They seek union with others and the world around them.

- A peacemaker does not like expectations or pressure. If you want him to do something, how you ask is important. He likes to listen and be of service, but do not take advantage of this. He is very easy to deal with if given time to finish things and make decisions. He likes a good discussion but not a confrontation. He is very caring and concerned about others. He is a good mediator and facilitator; has heightened awareness of sensations, aesthetics, is non-judgmental and accepting.
- A peacemaker faces problems when he is being judged or is misunderstood as indecisive. He is sensitive to criticism, taking every raised eyebrow and twitch of the mouth personally. He may be confused about what he really wants and worry too much about what others will think of him.

Example: The Indian Prime Minister Atal Bihari Vajpayee has the peace maker type of personality, who is receptive and can run a government supported by different groups in the parliament.

There is another classification of personality types. The style or the behavioural personality traits are made up of a few important elements. The elements of a personality are **conflict solving, initiative, inquiry, advocacy,**

decision-making and critique. All these six elements can give different shapes to personalities. We can explore how these six elements can determine the type of personality you have. To get this query solved you may attempt to undertake the following exercise:

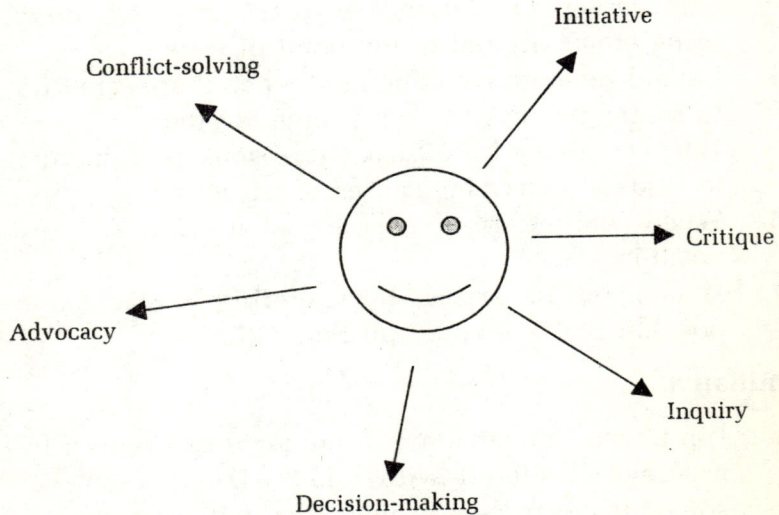

Exercise 1
Evaluation sheet of your style

The elements of a personality are briefly described in the following sections. Rank the sentences from 7 down to 1 where 7 represents the sentence within each element that you feel typifies your own personality the most.

Conflict Solving

1. I maintain a neutral stance or try to stay out of conflict altogether.
2. When conflict arises, I shift and turn in an effort to get around it; I avoid getting caught head on.
3. When conflict arises, I acknowledge it but re-emphasise the importance of what I propose to do to bring others around to my point of view.
4. I avoid generating conflict, but when it appears I try to soothe feelings to keep people together.
5. When conflict arises, I seek out reasons for it in order to resolve underlying causes of tensions.
6. When conflict arises, I try to cut it off or win my position.
7. When conflict arises, I try to find a reasonable position that everyone can live with.

Initiative

1. I initiate actions that are in my own best interest by seeking a trade-off with others. I help them get something that they want if they will help me get something I want.
2. I seek to maintain a steady pace and confine my effort to the tried and true.
3. I put out enough to get by, generally in response to requests from others.
4. I exert vigorous effort and others enthusiastically join in.
5. I expect others to follow my lead and extend positive appreciation to those who support my efforts.

6. I drive others and myself.
7. I initiate whatever actions might help and support the efforts of others.

Inquiry

1. I dig out areas of vital private concern to me in an inquisitive but non-threatening way.
2. I expect others to keep me informed and I show appreciation when they do; I look with disfavour upon those who fail to keep me up to date.
3. I search for and seek to verify information. I also invite and listen to ideas and attitudes different than my own.
4. I continuously treat the soundness of my own thinking by comparing it with the thinking of others.
5. I stay on top of information to be sure that I am in control and double-check everything I hear to be sure that others are not making mistakes.
6. I search for information that suggests all is well. For the sake of harmony, I am not inclined to challenge what others say.
7. I solicit information in order to see where others stand on an issue; this lets me know whether my thinking is on track.

Advocacy

1. I keep my own counsel but respond to questions when asked. I rarely reveal my convictions because then I do not have to stand behind them.
2. I tell others what they want or expect to hear.

3. I express my convictions in a tentative way and try to meet others half way.
4. I feel it is important to express my concerns and convictions in order that others know what I am thinking. I respond to ideas sounder than my own by changing my mind.
5. I stand up for my convictions because I know I am right. If others oppose me, I try to prove them wrong.
6. I embrace the ideas of others even though I may have private reservations. I feel it's better to be supportive than right.
7. Although I seldom back off my own convictions, I do permit others to express their ideas so I can understand where they are coming from and help them see the error of their thinking.

Decision-making

1. I search for decisions that maintain good relations and encourage others to make the decisions for me when possible.
2. Although I seek the final say in decisions, I still listen to what others have to say. In this way they get the benefit of my thinking, but I maintain their loyalty.
3. I let others make decisions or else leave it to fate.
4. I lobby my points of view to others in order to 'sell' my position; I may use persuasion or indirect threats to ensure that my wishes are carried out.
5. I search for workable decisions that others find acceptable.
6. I place high value on arriving at sound decisions; I

seek input from others and work for understanding and agreement.
7. I place high value on making my own decisions and am rarely influenced by what others have to say.

Critique

1. I pinpoint weaknesses or failure to measure up; in the event of a mistake, I assess blame.
2. I give encouragement and offer praise when something positive happens but avoid saying anything negative.
3. When I give feedback to others, I expect them to appreciate it because it is for their own good.
4. I avoid giving feedback and rarely critique the work of others or myself.
5. I use critique to motivate and inspire others to further the action that is in my best interest; I tend to discount negative aspects of performance as this lowers the level of enthusiasm.
6. I give informal or indirect feedback to keep others moving forward at an acceptable pace; if I have to say something negative, I make sure I have something positive to say as well.
7. I encourage two-way feedback to strengthen operations. I place high value on critique and it is evidenced in everything I do.

Theories of Personality Development

Erikson, the famous psychologist, has suggested that we can divide the personality of a man into nine different stages. The development and growth of an infant to a full-grown person has these nine stages as per his theory. For this book we shall limit our reading to two stages—stage 5 and stage 6—that is, between the age group of 12-40.

Stage 5: Adolescence, that is, age 12 to 18 is the age when a person is undergoing a Crisis of Identity versus Role Confusion. That is the time when we ask the question "Who am I?" To successfully answer this question, Erikson suggests, the adolescent must integrate the healthy resolution of all earlier conflicts. Did we develop the basic sense of trust? Do we have a strong sense of independence, competence, and feel in control of our lives? Adolescents who have successfully dealt with earlier conflicts are ready for the "Identity Crisis" which is considered by Erikson as the single most significant conflict a person must face.

The positive outcome of this stage is that if the adolescent solves this conflict successfully, he will come out of this stage with a strong identity and will be ready to plan for the future. But there may be some negative outcomes too and if so, the adolescent will sink into confusion, unable to make decisions and choices, especially about vocation, sexual orientation, and his role in life in general.

Stage 6: Young Adulthood, age 19 to 40, the crisis is Intimacy versus Isolation. This is the stage when the most important events are love relationships. No matter how successful you are with your work, said Erikson, you are not developmentally complete until you are capable of intimacy. An individual who has not developed a sense of identity usually will fear a committed relationship and may retreat into isolation. The positive outcome of this stage is that adults can form close relationships and share with others if they have achieved a sense of identity. The negative outcome is that if they have not found this identity, they will fear commitment, feel isolated and be unable to depend on anybody in the world.

Freud has identified Psychosexual Stages of Development. According to Sigmund Freud, what we do and why we do it, who we are and how we become this way are all related to our sexual drive. Differences in personalities originate from differences in childhood sexual experiences. Many of the behavioural scientists may not agree with his views.

Alfred Adler studied personality around the time of Sigmund Freud and Carl Jung, but developed very different ideas. Although he changed his theory many times during his lifetime, he always believed that people had control over their lives and made choices concerning themselves. He named his theory 'Individual Psychology' because he felt each person was unique and no previous theory applied to all people. *Adler's theory is comprised primarily of four aspects: striving towards superiority, the unity of personality, the development of personality, and psychological health, which includes intervention.*

Adler's theory of personality covers many aspects, including: what drives people, how the mind works to achieve goals, how personality is developed, and what constitutes mental health. Adler strongly disagreed with his precursors and peers because his theory revolved around the notion that *one has control over one's life.*

Personality Development – What are the Right Moves?

The world is getting tougher and with globalisation becoming a reality executives need to be smarter and polished enough to take up responsibilities with confidence and self-awareness. The personality factor has proved to be the key to modern corporate and business success. The most important prerequisite for such success is Personality with a capital P. It is true that not everyone is born with presence and style. "Personality re-engineering" can do the needful. Personality re-engineering helps groom the new generation executives and provides a finishing touch along with mannerisms, etiquette, diction and stress management. These days, most institutes as well as corporate houses are emphasising personality development courses in their curriculum. The course on personality development can help a person in the following ways:

- To learn the business etiquette of exchanging cards, wishing on first meeting, bowing when you are visiting Japan, and the like.
- Voice modulation, diction, communication skills, phone etiquette, hygiene, empowerment skills, time management and positive thinking.
- To cultivate a friendly, interactive manner. Essentials like giving a speech, voice development and modulation of voice.
- Personality development can help teach a marketing executive the art of convincing clients with charm and well-presented arguments.

- Personal projection is done with personality development. All other things remaining equal, personal projection is what makes or breaks a commercial relationship.
- Every person can realise his full potential. The personality development course helps in enhancing the sense of confidence and self-worth.

The veteran personality trainer, Sabira Merchant, puts it in her own words, "There is a demand for professionals who are perfect and polished, so more and more people in business circles want to be better."

Components of Personality

Different people have different opinions about what makes a man's personality complete. There are several behavioural scientists who have the view point that character does not form a part of personality, but Steven Covey, one of the all-time great authors and motivators, says that the best of behavioural traits fail if they are not based on the solid foundation of character.

Three Elements of Success

The Indian management guru, Arindam Chaudhuri, has come up with the concept of three basic elements for accomplishing any task effectively. He terms it as **ASK** (attitude, knowledge and skill). These three elements are essential in the right proportions to achieve the desired success.

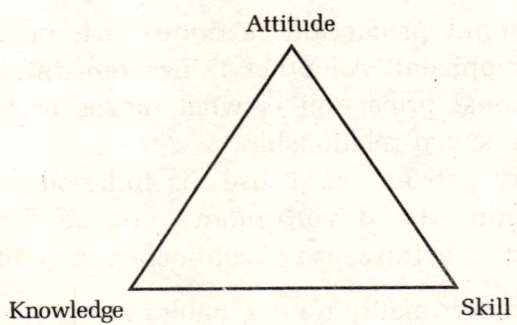

Let us take an example. An athlete who wants to win a gold medal in the Olympics must be **skilful** in the first instance. He must sharpen his skills with regular and rigorous practice. But practice alone cannot make him suitable for becoming a champion at that level. He must acquire the **knowledge** of intricate details. Apart from this, he must also posses the latest techniques in the track and the field arena. He must analyse the weakness and strength of all his opponents. He can win this race if he starts thinking that he is representing a country that has never been able to prove its mettle at that level. If he is to become a champion, his **attitude** must also be that of a champion. He must see it as the opportunity to grab the attention of people and achieve his target. Thus, a right proportion of these three elements is essential for achieving targets.

The other famous motivator and behavioural scientist, **Shiv Khera**, has propagated the **Theory of Four Ds** for success. He says that determination, direction, dedication and desire are the four main factors for anyone to succeed. In spite of better intelligence and potential the real winner will be the one who has an abundance of the four Ds mentioned above.

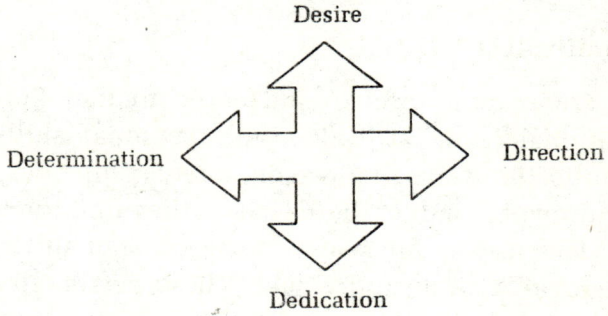

The person who wants to improve his personality has to have **desire** and **determination**; he has to identify the **direction** for his goals to achieve it. Once all the above three steps are taken he has to **dedicate** himself to the task of achieving his goal.

We need to develop personality traits that are very unique. Blindly following someone else who is successful will never take you in the direction right for you.

"If I am not for myself, who will be?"
—Pirke Avoth

"To be nobody else but yourself – in a world which is doing its best, night and day, to make you everybody else – means to fight the hardest battle any human being can fight, and never stop fighting."

—E.E. Cummings, American Author

> "Every man is unique and he has his peculiar ambition." —Abraham Lincoln

Personality Test

There are several tests to judge the mental aptitude, motivational level, attitude, inter personal skills and communication skills of a person. Many companies, prior to recruitment, conduct these tests as they find the formal way of face-to-face interviews not good enough to judge the personality of an individual. These personality tests are done in a controlled environment. The personality tests can identify an individual's:

- value system,
- emotional reaction to a critical situation,
- moods and characteristic behaviour traits,
- maturity in handling a crisis,
- ability to adjust himself to the stress of day-to-day executive lifestyle,
- self-confidence, personal ambition, emotional control and sociability etc.

To assess some of the behavioural traits such as impulsiveness, emotional reaction, fear, patience, distrust, optimism, initiative and leadership capability, the companies generally conduct these tests. This can be used for the selection of the right candidate who can handle difficult situations with ease.

For example: A company is recruiting a Construction Supervisor for a project of a fly-over construction in

Kolkata. The person has to control a group of fifty skilled and unskilled personnel and look after a host of construction materials and T&Ps (Tools and Plants). In a normal situation, a person who will be selected for the post of Construction Supervisor will have to apply very little technical knowledge that he has learnt in college, but he must be a good human resource manager with the ability to handle agitating and adamant workers. The company would like to recruit a person with *an average intelligence*, but with the *suitable personality traits* to match the job requirement.

There are three types of personality tests, which are conducted by several companies. We may like to know what they are intended for and how they are conducted.

Objective tests: These tests are conducted to assess the level of irrational tendencies in a person that arise in a not so conducive working environment. A person may not always get a working environment where all his subordinates are co-operative of his endeavour. These tests indicate the self-confidence of the person and also help in assessing the domination and submission of the person.

Projective tests: These are some of the tests in which a person is required to interpret the situation or react to a stimulus. The response of the person to these stimuli will indicate the person's motives, values and his personality in total. When we are required to react to such a situation, we always try to interpret it in a way we deem is right as per our own value. The results will be biased if the person conducting the test has indicated his own view.

Situational tests: These assess a person's capability of handling stress. These tests are conducted in a room with no identified leader to guide it to structured discussions. The discussion is allowed to take its own course and people are allowed to come out freely and openly to express themselves. People generally behave spontaneously in such an environment.

Case Study I

Ankit Kapur, 32, is the Country Manager of a multinational cosmetic company. The company is planning to launch a new range of products in India. The Asia Pacific Director, Robertson, is currently in India to review the prospect of producing the cosmetics in the Indian factory at Nasik. Ankit is a Chemical Engineer from IIT, Mumbai, with an excellent academic background. He was employed with the Research and Development wing of HLL till he left it to join the MNC at an attractive salary. Robertson is an executive who believes in statistics. Ankit prepared a presentation with well-researched statistics that showed a clear advantage of producing the cosmetics in the Indian factory.

The presentation was organised in a comfortable and serene five-star hotel conference room. The powerpoint presentation was done on the Video Projection System through the multimedia presentation stored in the laptop hard disk. This was a new experience for Ankit as he was not used to giving business presentations in his earlier job. He asked his second-in-command, Ravi, to be present in the conference room with all the necessary details. The hesitation and lack of experience in giving a presentation was more than evident when he began. Ankit was not following the sequence and kept on shifting from one point to another without any clue. Within a few minutes Robertson was thoroughly confused. He was not sure of the project. He left India saying that initially he was convinced that the Indian project was a feasible one, but Ankit's presentation showed more of the negative side rather than the advantages. The decision was kept on hold.

Ankit too was not happy with his communication skills. He joined a professional training course to improve his skills in presentation. In two months he was very confident and wanted to repair the damages done in the last presentation. In Paris, when he finished the presentation in front of the entire company board, the board was more than convinced that the project was not only feasible but highly profitable too. The difference in these two months was not because of any change in government policy in India or the investment strategy of the MNC, but the change in Ankit's presentation style.

Questions:

1. Can the presentation style change the fate of an investment?
2. Was Ankit's presentation full of data and statistics a right decision?

Section I
BEHAVIOURAL TRAITS

2

Communication Skills

Communication is the process of sharing information, ideas and opinions. It is a part and parcel of our daily routine. The sender sends the message and the receiver receives it at the other end. The message is passed on from one end to the other and the effect it has created on the receiver is obtained through the feedback. The desired effect of communication can be assessed properly if it is transmitted in the right medium and the meaning is decoded properly.

Allen, the famous behavioural scientist, says, "It (communication) involves a systematic and continuing process of telling, listening and undertaking."

Communication at any level and in any form involves two persons or parties. The first person that sends a message (verbal, written, gesture or non-verbal) is called the sender. The person who receives it is called the receiver. In most cases communication is two-way. The sender also has to play the role of the receiver in the reverse direction of communication. TV programmes, radio messages and news, written communication (in the form of letter, fax, or e-mail) is one-way till the reply of the same is not received. Similarly, verbal communication in a meeting is a two-way communication. Every message has a particular intention behind it and if the intended message and the received perception are the same the communication is said to be effective. At times, the message gets distorted due to noise in the channel of communication. If the channel-noise disturbs the communication, the message received will be affected.

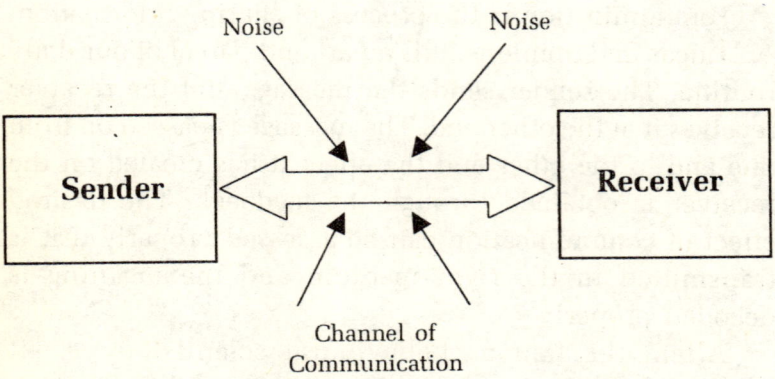

There may be several sources of and various channels of communication. Verbal communication can be between two people, face-to-face or through telephone or video conferencing. Communication can get distorted due to noise and the meaning may change drastically in such cases. Effective communication requires the reduction of the noise level.

Communication for Effectiveness

The best of skills and competency levels do not help if the communication is weak. Communication is important in business for success, but it is equally important for an individual to succeed. In a few of the studies conducted in large organisations, it has been established that more than 60 per cent of the time of an executive is spent in communicating. Whereas, in the case of top-level executives it may even exceed 80 per cent of their daily working time.

Peter Drucker has identified communication as the most important parameter in the effectiveness of a manager; he has listed the importance of communication very high in a priority list. Other functions of a manager, i.e. planning, organising, directing and controlling will be badly affected if communication is ineffective. It has been rightly said that **information dissemination is the single most important factor for the success of any business.**

Communication: How it works

The communication process has three basic elements—sender, receiver and message. Without these three elements no communication is possible. The process is not so simple, as there are other phenomena of coding, decoding and channels involved, and most important of all noise that is generated in all the channels.

The communication model given below shows the simplest possible way of the working of the communication process.

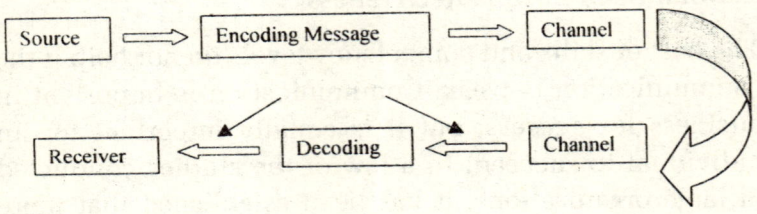

1. **Source:** This is the originating point in the communication process. The thought process is converted to a message, which is intended to reach the receiver. The source devises the message to convey needs, ideas and/or information.
2. **Encoding Message:** If the thoughts are not enough to convey the message from the sender to the receiver they are to be converted into a form that is understood by the receiver. This can be done with the help of some language or other ways of encoding the needs, thoughts and information like gestures and body language.
3. **Channels of Communication:** There are many ways we can send the encoded message from the sender to the receiver. The medium through which the message is sent is called the channel of communication. Audio and visual are the most common channels of communication, but there are other ways too, such as written memos, circulars, group meetings, public shows, television, newspaper, radio etc. We need to

identify the channel based on the requirement, like to whom is the message directed and what is the desired impact of the message.
4. **Receiver:** The message that has been sent by the sender has to be received by a receiver for the communication process to be complete. If the message is not received, the process remains incomplete.
5. **Decoding:** Just like the encoding of the message by the sender, the receiver of the message has to decode the message so that the intended message can be understood. The receiver has to interpret, understand and translate the message into a form that is understood by him.
6. **Feedback:** It is the response of the receiver to the sender. This is useful to the sender in assessing the outcome of the communication. As has been already said that communication is a two-way process, the absence of the receiver renders this process incomplete and ineffective.
7. **Noise:** The accuracy of the message communicated is badly affected by the noise in the communication. Noise is the factor that disturbs, confuses and interferes with the message communicated. It may distort the message considerably or may completely change its meaning, thus hindering the communication process.

Example: A baby boy (**the sender**) starts crying due to hunger. He is the source or originator of the message. His crying is the **encoded message** that is received by his mother (**the receiver**) and the **channel** is audio/verbal in nature as sound is used. The mother tries to understand the meaning of this crying by **decoding the message** in it. She soon realises that her baby is hungry and hence understands the message the correct way. As a result of this understanding, she prepares milk for the baby (**feedback**). Since the baby cannot talk, the mother has to try and decipher his reason for crying. This may act as the **noise** in the channel. She may misunderstand the reason for the crying to be an aching stomach. This is due to the noise in the form of non-clarity of message.

Barriers of Communication

Peter Drucker has said, "Although we attempt for good communication, but still it has proved as elusive as a unicorn.... the noise level has gone up so high that all we can listen to is the babbles of noise." We need to take these words very seriously to understand the gravity of the situation and the need and importance of bridging this communication gap.

There are plenty of examples in human history that show how communication got distorted in the process and an altogether different message got delivered when it reached its final destination. The reasons for such poor communication can be listed as follows:

1. **Semantic barrier:** A certain symbol or word may have a totally different meaning in a different country, place or region. Also, certain symbols may mean different things to different people by virtue of their subjective

perceptions. The failure to understand these connotations creates problem in communication. Such barrier in communication is known as semantic barrier.

Example: In Japan a person bows down to pay respect to the other person, but it means nothing in America and the gesture may be treated as foolish.

2. **Psychological barrier:** The meaning or decoding of the message will only be right if it is understood in the right frame of mind. The psychological barrier is very common in cases where the persons have different status and different emotional conditions such as fear, anger, anxiety or happiness.

Example: If a person is angry with someone he may use a taunting smile for greeting the other person as a gesture to hurt and insult him.

3. **Organisational barrier:** There are some fixed channels for the communication to be routed in an organisation. The letter from a MD is written formally only to the head of the department even if it is meant and required for a Supervisor. The Supervisor will get the message only as interpreted by the Manager. These formal channels in an organisation act as a barrier.

Importance of Informal Communication or Grapevine

Any information or opinion of a company/institute cannot be acquired from the formal channels that an organisation has devised for its employees/students, they get it from some other source. If there is news of interest to the workers it will spread in the mill without its appearing on the notice board. Such informal information is termed as grapevine. There are several other channels of spreading grapevine. Many times, companies use this informal channel to spread some of the information as this is flexible, has a personal touch and, more importantly, it has tremendous speed and does not cost the company.

Letter and its Importance in Communication

In our day-to-day life, for our personal exchange of opinions, ideas and information, we primarily rely on verbal communication. It is sufficient to verbally communicate a message, but in the office, letters, e-mails and fax play a more important role in conveying the official message. The demand for any message in writing is due to the fact that it can be kept as a record for future reference. Verbal communication does not solely depend on the language and it does not need structuring. The background need not be stated in verbal communication, but in written letters the structure and the language used are very important to make it effective. Body language and gestures are important aspects in verbal communication. All these aspects mentioned must be kept in mind to make communication effective.

There are several tools for written communication. Some of these tools are letters, applications, circulars, orders, notices, inter-office memos, notes etc. We can categorise communication on the basis of the function of the message in two different ways.

1. **Formal and Informal Communication:** The objective of communication, in terms of the message it intends to convey, will decide whether it is a formal or an informal communication. If you want to convey a congratulatory letter to your colleague, it will fall in an informal category, but if you place an order for the office stationery requirement to the materials section, it is formal communication. Formal communication is more structured and is drafted well before sending. It lacks personal touch and is intended for business purposes. In such communication we need to present a professional approach and avoid being too emotional, critical, harsh or poetic while expressing our needs. The language used for such formal official communication is more or less governed by a set pattern. Whereas, an informal letter can reflect the personality of the individual sending the written communication.
2. **Downward, Upward and Horizontal Communication:** A hierarchy exists in an office and the communication pattern will change depending upon who is addressing whom. Communication can be addressed to the boss for getting permission to avail casual leave. Such communication will be full of words of modesty and request. Whereas, when a person is writing to his subordinate for issuing the instruction for sending the monthly sales figures to the regional office, the tone, the words and the language must reflect authority and command. Similarly, we need to have a different approach for different people in view of our distinct

relations with friends and colleagues. Any communication addressed to an individual higher in the hierarchy than oneself is upward communication, to a subordinate is downward communication and to the peer group is horizontal communication.

Skills of Written Communication

The most powerful form of communication for business as well as personal purposes when the two persons/parties are far apart is written communication. Written communication is mostly in the form of letters, fax or e-mail. Whatever the medium of conveying the message the important thing is that it must convey the intended message, create goodwill and improve the relationship. It is rightly said, 'it is impossible to take back the words once spoken', but it is all the more difficult to repair the damage done by bitter, rude and malicious letters. The basic features of a good written communication are:

1. **The language should be simple.**
   Technical jargon, difficult phraseology or flowery language can impress anyone, but this does not mean everyone can use it with the same level of ease or accuracy. We may be good at it, but it is not the kind of language that must be extensively used in letter writing. The basic objective of conveying the message should not be lost.
2. **The style must be lucid, but effective.**
   The writer of the letter is not physically present when the letter is being read. The letter carries with it the

impression of the writer's style and personality. In many cases the letter is the stepping stone to forming good and lasting relationships and thus must convey the message in such a way that the meaning does not change or get distorted.

3. **The contents should be sober with depth of feeling and emotions.**

   A letter should never be written in a bad mood. Howsoever one may try, the negativity of the mood tends to creep into what one writes which may completely or partially change the meaning of the message.

4. **The letter should be comprehensive.**

   The importance of time ought to be respected, be it your own or the other person's. In this fast paced world, comprehensively written letters are welcome.

Case study II

Mrs Maini, 38, was a qualified secretarial staff in a Mumbai based MNC. She got married to a business executive in Delhi and was forced to shift to Delhi leaving her job after marriage. When she resigned and was leaving the company in Mumbai, she had an unpleasant discussion with her boss and HR personnel regarding the separation benefits. Her separation from the company was marred due to bad feelings and lack of understanding.

In Delhi, she was not happy sitting without any work at home. After a few months she noticed that her competence and speed with regards to operating the computer and typing had deteriorated. She talked to her husband and he agreed to her proposal of taking up another job in Delhi. Mrs Maini applied in several companies stating the problem and the reason why she left the job. But most companies seemed sceptical recruiting a married lady for secretarial jobs. One morning she saw a job advertisement for the post of Hospital Administration Secretary. She was not experienced for such a job, but she thought of trying something different.

This time she did not send her resume with any indication of her urgency to get a job. She drafted the letter with a different theme altogether starting with why there is a need of change in the attitude of the Hospital Administration people. She emphasised the need to bring in new innovative ideas to avoid the sick look of Indian private hospitals. She further suggested few of the administrative and housekeeping tips MNCs are acquainted with. Nowhere in the letter did she mention her compulsions of leaving her previous job and her eagerness to get this one. In the last paragraph she proposed herself as a candidate who could bring in the necessary changes. Surprisingly enough, the very next day she got a call from the HR Manager and they fixed an appointment for an interview the next day. The interview went well and Mrs Maini was selected and asked to join her new assignment within a week.

Questions:

1. Was the separation tussle a right move by Mrs Maini?
2. Is the concept of a married woman not suitable for office jobs in India the right approach?
3. Why did the hospital administration select Mrs Maini whereas others rejected her?

3

Sharpen Your Communication Skills

You may have good knowledge of your field, excellent skills and volumes of potential, but the world will know about all these only if you can properly present yourself as well as the qualities you have. Most people fail in competitions due to lack of effective communication skills. This is more important in cases of selection through interview and personality test. When we talk about communication we are not talking about any language skill. People generally perceive the lack of command of any particular language as their weakness. The lack of communication is more due to certain basic lacking in the behavioural pattern being followed and not due to the language being used.

Three major segments need to be worked upon to enhance communication skills:

1. Written communication
2. Verbal communication
3. Body Language

    The Indian management guru, Arindam Chaudhuri has very rightly said in his book, 'Verbal communication contributes only 33 per cent to the gamut of communication. The rest 67 per cent is all about listening and no one tells this better than nature itself. That we have two ears and one mouth probably means that nature means for us to listen twice as much as we speak.' Therefore, we can say that although listening is not a direct category in the classification mentioned above, it is one of the most important ingredients for effective communication. Very vital to start with, this is an area where there is tremendous scope for improvement and the results are more than visible. Take for instance the transformation in the communication skills of well-known cricketers like Mohd Azharuddin and Kapil Dev. On the other hand we are very impressed by the way the likes of Aishwarya Rai and Sushmita Sen talk, seldom realising the fact that a tremendous amount of hard work, training and effort has gone into achieving that result.

    People having good communication skills generally win the race as soon as it begins. It is said that the first thirty seconds of interaction with any person creates an impression that lasts forever. So these thirty seconds are very critical and we need to prepare for such interactions beforehand.

    We would like to see where and how we can improve upon our communication skills and what are the basic areas that need to be avoided to tackle undesired situations.

What is Body Language and Postures?

The most powerful of all the languages is the language one's body speaks. Even when we are not communicating verbally, we keep on communicating through our actions and postures. The unwritten rules and codes may not be the same everywhere in the world, but with this unique language you can convey your feeling, reaction, need and attitude wherever you go. To master this language, you need to practise it and improve upon it. This is an integral part of personality development.

Body language is not an exact science. Sometimes a person's movement or gestures can be guided by his subconscious thoughts or emotions, but more often clues can be wrong.

According to Michael Argyle of Oxford University, 'non-verbal signals are used to establish and maintain personal relationships, while words are used to communicate information about external events.'

Studying body language does not make you a mind-reader. Another person's body just sends signals to your subconscious and that is why it is such a powerful form of communication.

Example: A friend of yours is going out for a movie and asks you to join. You may not reply in words, but simply shake your head in negativity. That is body language.

Body Language

We tend to judge people more from the way they look than what they actually say to us. But this judgment is largely subconscious. We rarely stop to analyse why we form a certain opinion about someone. If we try and analyse it, we will often find it based on prejudice. When we meet someone, body language helps in making the first impression.

Balanced view: Just think of your own posture while you are reading this book? If you are sitting in a relaxed pose it speaks volumes about how much you are at home with the subject of this book.

Have you ever thought how you look like when in a particular posture? If someone just enters the room and meets you for the first time, he will form an opinion about you by looking at you. The first few seconds are the most important for the formation of that vital image. Try to analyse the same by answering the following questions:

1. Are your legs and hands folded?
2. Do you stare at someone when he enters the room?
3. Do you welcome the person who has just entered by standing up and stretching your hand to greet him?
4. Do you continue slumped in the chair?
5. Do you show any interest in his introductory wishes?

Body language communicates much more than words. Thus, it is more useful if we try to find what our unsaid words communicate to others and whether what our body language communicates is what we intend to say.

You are at a party curled up in a chair with arms crossed and frowning. You must not wonder why no one in the party talks to you. You are intentionally or unintentionally giving a message that you want to be left alone. Nobody will come and ask for explanations from you.

What we are trying to emphasise here is that working on body language is an effective way of improving your personality. A person should be aware how certain postures and body languages are generally perceived and decoded. There should be an effort on the part of the person to assume a posture that is reflective of his feelings.

Purists may feel that it is incorrect to conceal negative feelings under the mask of body language. Body language can act as a protective armour if used more correctly.

Example: When you go for an interview, but lack confidence your body language will send out a negative signal that you are unsure of yourself. When the people on the deciding panel see that signal they react to it. If they see a confident signal they will react in a different way. If people treat you as though you are confident, you begin to feel you are.

Leakage: Body language signals are called 'leakages' because you may try to tell something, but the truth will leak out visually.

Example: Imagine you are appearing for an interview. You are asked how you find yourself suitable for the job. You may be saying that you have the confidence to undertake the job, but all the time your leg is moving to and fro and you keep fiddling with your hair. These negative signals will be seen as leaking out messages that belie your words.

Avoid Such Body Language

When a person is appearing for an interview, he/she may be nervous and the body language may not match the words uttered by the person. Few negative leakages have been identified that you should try to avoid, like:

- crossed arms or legs
- carrying books or papers across your chest
- slumped posture
- sitting perched on the edge of the chair
- wringing hands
- tapping foot
- rocking legs
- drumming fingers
- biting nails
- fiddling with the jewellery or hair
- covering your mouth with your hand while talking
- rocking in your chair
- scratching a lot
- clearing your throat too much
- straightening your tie
- playing with watch or cufflinks
- hands in the pocket

Looking aggressive: The body posture may also show a defiant stance of the person. Few of the very common postures that can lead to a situation of conflict may be avoided if we change our behaviour and body language, which may be in use, like:

- arms folded across the chest
- staring

- pointing
- making a fist
- leaning over someone

Behaving rudely: When you talk about all the nice and pleasant things, your actions, too, should be in the same frame of reference. Many times rudeness is reflected in our behaviour. We can improve our personality to a great extent if we can avoid such behaviour:

- working when someone is talking to you
- puffing
- tottering
- smirking
- whispering
- cracking knuckles
- grooming yourself
- standing too close

Rudeness during meetings: During several official meetings people tend to act as if they are not interested in continuing with the meeting. We must avoid such negative signals in those cases:

- packing up folders and papers well before the meeting is over
- shaking hands too hard or limp handshakes
- yawning when the meeting is in progress
- looking at your watch repeatedly

Pet fiddles: We all have some pet fiddles that we indulge in without even noticing ourselves. What are these? These are nothing but nervous comfort gestures. When other people notice such things about us and inform us of the same, it comes as a shock. For an overall development of personality such fiddling habits need to be got rid of, like:

- blinking a lot
- fiddling with rings, watches, earrings and chains
- tapping or clicking pens
- playing with paper clips
- jingling money in pocket
- picking at fingernails
- twiddling bits of hair
- smoking

You may not do these things because you are nervous, but they will make you look so, all the same.

How to Apply This Tip

The way to improve these negative traits is to identify such negative gestures and try not to repeat them at moments when it counts. Say, if you are facing an interview or attending a meeting you must be in a position to identify the gesture that can land you in a disadvantageous position. The best place to find the solution is to go to a friend or a colleague and they will be more than pleased to help you out.

MASTER THE ART OF PLEASANT GESTURES

A lot of us speak with our hands. Some people claim they cannot talk at all if their arms are clamped down to their sides. Gestures can be useful as long as we have control over our conversation. If gestures endorse our words they will add emphasis and interest. If they act as leakages contradicting our desired message then we are in trouble.

Example: A TV news anchor, as part of her job, needs to tell news that may be good or bad. Her gestures must complement what she is saying. If she is reading about the sad demise of a veteran leader with a smile on her face or is sad while informing of the great Indian victory over the English cricket team, it may cast a doubt on the communication skills of the anchor.

When people see themselves on TV they are surprised by what they see. Often we do not recognise ourselves on the screen. That is because we see ourselves as others see us for the very first time. It is a shock and very rightly so.

We see our arms waving like windmills or our feet tapping out some sub-conscious rhythm and we come up with the classic comment, "I did not know I did that!" The trouble is, others did. Colleagues have known for years, only we were ignorant. We use the famous ostrich technique—stick our head in the sand. We make an effort to ignore it, not look at it and will it to go away—right?

Of course, the fact is that if we refuse to acknowledge these gestures they will not go away at all—it's just that we won't see them again. The more sensible line is to find out all we can about such habits of ours and see what needs keeping and what needs editing.

Our bodies should dance in tune with our words. When the words we speak and the gestures we make fall out of step, its time to rethink. Gestures, if too persistent, can be irritating to others. They will also be annoying if they look too pompous.

There are, in addition, gestures that are 'trendy' and can be as aggravating as trendy words. Like, when did you last see someone hanging air quotes round every other word?

Pompous Gestures (Self important or Arrogant)—To be avoided.

- Head tilted back when you talk.
- Eyes closed when you talk.
- Looking down your nose.
- Peering over the top of your glasses.
- Waving glasses about when you talk.
- Pursed mouth.

Daft (Silly) Gestures—To be avoided.

- Flapping hands around as you talk.
- Undoing and then doing up jacket buttons or watchstraps.
- Chains that you put in the mouth or rest over the chin or the nose.
- Wringing hands.
- Wiping your face on your shirt's sleeve.
- Tearing paper into little bits.
- Cleaning ears or nails while talking to someone.
- Banging the table instead of laughing when someone tells a joke.
- Shoes hanging off toe or off feet altogether.
- Chewing pens.

- Air quotes, thumbs up or any gesticulation meaning some obscene remark.

Positive Gestures — Must try these.
- Open hand gestures.
- Carrying documents to one side, rather than clutched to the chest.
- Keeping the thumb out when you put your hands in your pockets—that way you won't stuff them too far inside.
- Good listening gestures—eye contact, tilting the head, nodding to encourage speech, leaning forward slightly to indicate interest.

Useful Gestures

Gestures can help us be polite when we are unable to speak. For instance, if you are busy on the phone and visitors arrive, you can acknowledge them politely with a nod and maybe one finger held up to show 'one minute!' instead of ignoring them till you are free.

Gestures can also be used to show assertiveness. If a colleague constantly interrupts you while you are on the phone, you might raise the flat of your hand towards him in a 'stop' gesture to get him to wait. Whereas, if you just look away, he may try harder to interrupt.

Territory and Touch

We all have our invisible circle of territory around us and feel uncomfortable if someone we do not know breaches that circle. It's our space and we are fiercely defensive of it.

'Important' people tend to be allotted more personal space, which is why being part of a crowd can make us feel little and inferior, leading to anxiety or aggression. Invaded space is something we find impossible to talk about, however uncomfortable it may make us feel. In tests done in America, a volunteer deliberately sat within the 'comfort zone' of strangers in a public space. The reaction of those strangers was to turn away, display anxiety or even walk away completely. Not one person asked the volunteer to move.

When we move about, we move within four distance bands, each one defined by the discomfort level we feel when that band is breached.

- The farthest band is the **public band**. At this distance we are comfortable with most strangers. If talking in public this would be the distance at which you would feel most comfortable.
- Then comes the **social band**. This is the distance we keep while talking to people not very well known to us.
- The third band is the **friendly band**—the sort of gap we would keep between people and ourselves at a party or in a pub.
- The nearest band is the **intimate band**—and this is reserved for lovers and close family members.

When someone invades the wrong band or territory it makes us feel extremely uncomfortable, even if we make the effort to hide that discomfort.

The Rule of Privacy

When someone invades our intimate band without invitation we feel acute discomfort because the signals we receive indicate a sexual or physical threat. Our bodies prepare for the 'fight or flight' response—the breathing quickens, the heart starts pumping faster and the adrenalin pours into the bloodstream. To mask our discomfort we will often smile more. Interrogators often use similar techniques to browbeat their victim.

Only invade another's intimate space if you're absolutely sure it's appropriate. The friendly arm around the shoulder or seat pulled close may be done for the best of motives, but it could have disastrous results.

Your desk becomes part of that territory and so does your chair. You will feel annoyed and uncomfortable if someone puts his or her things on your desk or sits on your chair without asking.

We are forced to invade other people's territory everyday. Travelling to work on a crowded train or bus or getting into a full lift means we are too close for comfort—but we can cope with that as long as the subconscious body language rules are observed. To acknowledge you've invaded another's space and to show that you mean no threat, you stare into space and make minimal movement. People in the lift usually stand straight and look intently at the floor numbers. Commuters in a bus or train go out of their way not to make eye contact with one another.

Balance is vital in situations like this and any imbalance of eye contact, smiling, distance and leaning can lead to an approach and avoidance situation, where one party will be invasive while the other is forced into retreat. If we stand or sit too close to someone, we normally try to redress the balance by lessening other signs of intimacy, like eye contact. It is also forbidden to touch without permission, even accidentally. Two people brushing past each other will duly apologise for the inadvertent contact.

Hand-Shaking: An Excellent Business Gesture

Touch breaks down barriers, so a kind of 'permitted touching system' has been invented for business and social use. We use this in business via the handshake. It is the only form of touch considered appropriate, especially on a first meeting.

The handshake, then, becomes a loaded dice. Who extends his or her hand first? How strong should be the grip? Who do you shake hands with? Some men even think it inappropriate to shake hands with a woman. If you are nervous about meeting someone you will know all about the dreaded sweaty palm syndrome.

- In business it is the person doing the greeting who should instigate the handshake, or the one in the superior position. The handshake should always take place using the right hand and it should vary in firmness, depending on the one you are receiving. You should not grab someone's arm as you shake his or her hand and you should use eye contact.

- Two-handed shakes are a bit too earnest, especially on first meeting.
- Do not wipe a sweaty palm on the leg of your trousers or skirt just as you make your approach—a furtive dab with a tissue or some cologne is much more attractive.

Touch is variable according to culture and nationality. Sidney Jourard of Florida University watched people talking together in public and counted the times they touched in the space of one hour. In Puerto Rico it was 180, in Paris 110 and in London zero.

FACE—WHAT DOES IT SAY?

We know who is who by looking at his face, but the expression on your face tells what mood you are in. It is the mirror of your personality.

Of course you cannot see the look on your face because you are on the wrong side of your eyeballs. You may think you are looking wonderfully alert and intelligent, but other people may tell a different story. Facial expressions are even more open to misinterpretation than body language.

Facial expressions are important because it is the face we spend the most time looking at when we are talking to one another.

Can you hide your feelings?

We hide a lot more in business than we do in our social lives—trying to look interested when we are bored, knowledgeable when we do not have any clue, and polite when we dislike the person we are dealing with.

If your job means coping with the public on a daily basis, you will be well acquainted with qualities like tolerance and patience. We all have heard the phrase: 'The customer is always right.' What it means, of course, is that we have to pretend they are right, even when we know they are not. It is at this point that the corporate smile will come into play—and a fearsome sight it is, too.

Smiles that look false are dreadful. People who have to employ them on a regular, long-term basis—such as politicians and greeters at exhibitions—often end up displaying a terrifying gesture that drives clients away.

Smile and its Importance

A smile can win you what all the hard work could not win. It can take you to success where even your best efforts have failed to lead you. When an animal bares its teeth it is showing aggression—and it is what we unwittingly display if our smile looks fake. The teeth are on display, but the eyes are dead; the lights are on, but no one is at home.

If your job entails smiling through thick and thin, you should at least practise that grin until it becomes natural and sincere looking. The trick is to smile with your eyes as well as your mouth. Try it.

Most of us have two major facial expressions—smiling and miserable. Unfortunately, the older we get the more extreme these two become. Skin starts to droop, frown lines set in, laughter lines look like creases of utter misery. When we smile, the effort of lifting all the sagging flesh becomes greater each year.

Face-lifts—The Solution

Face-lifts may sound like the solution, but too many and too tight and they can stretch the skin back into a permanent expression of alarm.

All you have to do is to compensate. Look in the mirror a lot. Faces in repose will usually look miserable. Find ways of looking serious and business-like instead of depressed. Do not be embarrassed—actors do it, so why not you? Raise an eyebrow. Try looking amused. Now try cynical. Why not have a go at sexy? Feel the muscles working. Check out the results. Practise. See what looks good.

There is no dishonesty in a little self-discovery. It is much worse to look permanently worried or anxious without knowing it.

Seeing EYE-2-EYE

Eye contact is a powerful tool. Use too little and you will look nervous or even shifty. Use too much and you will appear overpowering and aggressive.

Looking people in the eye is a bit like breathing—it is something we do without thinking. But when it is brought to our attention we find it difficult to maintain.

How much eye contact do you use in business? Do a one-day check-up and you will be surprised at the results. Study the eye contact of your colleagues, too. Do they use more than you, or less? Do you use it more with some people than with others—if so, why? How much eye contact do you use when you are listening to people or greeting clients?

Like the strength of the handshake or the amount you smile, you will find your eye contact will vary depending on who you are dealing with.

Some people are hesitant to look straight in the eye—usually because they use either too much eye contact or not enough. If they spend most of their time with their eyes fixed on the floor during the conversation, with only quick glances in our direction, we tend to look at them less. If they stare us out, we feel embarrassed and look away more quickly.

During conversation people will look at one another on an average between one and two-thirds of the time and gazing not more than two-thirds of the time. If they spend more than two-thirds of the time gazing then chances are they are in love.

When you are made to feel uncomfortable by a conversation or question you will tend to look away, but if you become aggressive your eye contact will probably increase.

During a natural conversation we use more eye contact while listening than while speaking. This gives the impression we are listening intently and speaking honestly. If you look away when someone is talking to you, you give the impression of being bored by the conversation.

Sometimes our eyes stray out to some other parts of the face during a conversation. If we stay around the eye area we should be alright. Look at the mouth too much and you will either look as though you are flirting or studying a piece of spinach stuck between the other person's teeth.

Gaze at the end of the nose and you will bring out all sorts of paranoia in him or her.

Thus, eye contact has to be used, but in moderation, like most other things. Too much or too little tends to give signals other than intended.

Eye Contact Exercise

It is a good idea to use eye contact in business, especially if you lack confidence or assertive skills. The trick is not to overdo it, though. Try a few of these exercises to help to increase you eye contact more comfortably.

- Stare your dog out. (Yes, you might make him twitchy, but it's easier to start with pets than humans. If you cannot even meet the dog's gaze you will know you have serious insecurity problems.)
- Stare yourself out. Look in the mirror and tell yourself loudly that you are confident, really confident.
- Find a friend you feel comfortable with (no laughing) and take turns to ask and reply to some simple requests using eye contact. Then role-play more difficult situations, like asking for money or confessing to a ten-year affair with the friend's partner.
- When you greet someone new in business hold eye contact all the way through the verbal greeting and do not rush your words. Smile at the same time— you do not want to come across as aggressive.
- When you talk to colleagues call them by their names and do not start speaking until they have

met your gaze. (Do not be strict about this one. A more nervous colleague may feel uncomfortable. Try it on the more confident types first.)

Case study I

Govind Nayak is the Area Manager of the international telecommunications company Motorola. They are implementing a project to establish a fibre optic network in the city of Mumbai. The company has acquired the necessary permission from the Ministry of Telecommunication to lay cables in the city. To lay underground cables, permission from the local authorities for digging and cutting the road is required. Govind has co-ordinated with his company to send all tools and plants from his parent company and arranged a team of specialised workers from Chennai to undertake the job. The work was to commence this week, but the permission from the local administration is not forthcoming. The local district administration is not allowing the company to commence the work although all the papers required have already been furnished to the Municipal Council Administrator, Mr Govilkar. The team leader of the company informed Govind that the administrator was not happy with the company, as in one of the company's presentations to the State Government officials Govilkar was not invited. Govind made up his mind to meet Govilkar personally.

On the appointed day and time, when Govind went to the Administrator's office he had to wait for twenty-five minutes, after being informed at the reception that Govilkar was busy with some other meeting. Govind asked one of his team members to find out what he was actually doing and, to his surprise, he found the Administrator chatting with a few of his friends. When finally he was called Govilkar was looking at some papers and did not even bother to answer the introductory wish. He kept himself seated. Govind had to extend his hand and stretch to reach him for a handshake. When Govind started to tell his requirements and the permission from the municipal authority, he kept himself busy with some petty affairs. In the meantime, there was a telephone call from the local MLA and Govilkar spent a few minutes chatting with him. There were a few more calls during the meeting. Govilkar was mostly talking in terms of Ya's, Na's and Ummmphs. He never felt it necessary to see face to face with Govind and the team members. After fifteen minutes, the meeting came to an end with no assurance from Govilkar.

Govind was very upset with the behaviour and attitude of the administrator. He was thoroughly disgusted with the working of these departments and wanted to settle things once and for all. He sought an appointment with the IT Secretary of the State at three that afternoon. When Govind reached, he was allowed to go straight to the IT Secretary's room as instructions had been issued beforehand. The man was neatly dressed and seeing the team, got up from his chair and welcomed them. He was smiling and receptively listening to the problems being faced by the MNC. He instructed his PA not to allow anyone to disturb him for the next ten minutes. Not pleased with the way the Municipal Department was handling the case, he called the Chairman and asked to clear the permission on return fax. The stalemate was over within a few minutes with a slight dose of positive attitude and genuine effort to help the MNC in completing the project for the betterment of the city.

Questions:

1. What are the grey areas in the behaviour of the Administrator?
2. List your recommendations of simple gestures that could have changed the meeting environment.
3. What are your suggestions for better working in Government departments?

ART OF PRESENTATION

For any effective presentation we need to take up some homework prior to it. The behavioural scientist **Stephen Covey** has aptly said, 'Seek first to understand then to be understood'. Knowing how to be understood is equally critical in reaching a win-win solution.

To understand the presentation process better we can follow the three sequentially arranged words from Greek Philosophy: "Ethos, Pathos and Logos." These three words contain the essence of seeking first to understand and then making an effective presentation. Ethos is personal credibility—the faith people have in your integrity and competency. It's the trust that you inspire. Pathos is the empathic side—the feeling. It means that you are in alignment with the person with whom you are communicating. Logos is the logic, the reasoning part of the presentation.

The sequence should be ethos (your character), pathos (your relationship) and then logos (the reasoning of your presentation). Most people jump to the final step, without passing through the first two stages and land up in an unsuccessful sales presentation.

Effective presentation and public speaking are talents not every man is born with. But behavioural experts do believe that it is one area, which can be improved largely by practise. For any professional, effective presentation is a must. There are a few pointers that can be used to enhance the presentation skills of a person.

1. **Priming the mind** is vital. For a successful presentation, homework is important and the presenter must be sure of what he communicates.
2. **Logic based planning**: The planning must be done keeping in mind all probable questions and irritants, if any. The presenter must face unexpected or unwanted questions in a calm way and without losing his/her temper. Such answers need to be prepared better than the main agenda so that, when asked, a clear explanation can be given.
3. **Always avoid argument**: Arguments will not lead you to a favourable situation. If you win the argument, you will lose the goodwill and if you lose goodwill, you lose any way. Avoiding an argument is the best solution of an argument.

4. **Mental paradigm:** For any presentation there is a standard or model that the presenter must have in mind so as not to waver from the track.
5. **Audience interference:** At times the audience who have a fair bit of information about the subject will interfere, which must be handled patiently and without drawing oneself into argument. The answer should not be offensive.
6. **Overcoming stage fright:** Stage fright is present not only in a novice, but in highly accomplished speakers too. They also experience butterflies in their stomach before they face an audience. Prepare yourself for the presentation by having a few sips of water, stretching yourself, making faces in front of a mirror, or generally try putting yourself at ease.

The basic mantra for an effective presentation is **KISS (Keep It Small and Simple).** The focus should be the motivational and key messages and other details may be supplemented in writing.

The art of public speaking can be improved if we try these few tips given by expert orators:

1. Do not overload the presentation with unnecessary details.
2. If the presentation is in Powerpoint or OHP (Over Head Projector) slides, the fonts should be clear and big.
3. Take care not to overdo the slides. The pace of the knowledge sharing must be assessed.

4. If the group is not uniform in terms of demography and educational background, try to explore a subject of common interest.
5. Try to convey your message and not waste your effort in scoring points over someone.

Case Study I

Harish, a sales executive in an office automation company, had to present the new range of photocopy machines for a prospective customer, an MNC. As the company had to buy several of these machines, the VP of the company himself desired to be present during the presentation. Harish came in fifteen minutes late for the presentation, fully drenched in sweat. His helping hands followed him, rushing with the machine. He was in such a hurry to make up for the lost time that he almost tumbled down at the entrance of the conference room. He apologised for being late explaining that he was stuck in a routine traffic jam. The Administrative Manager introduced Harish to all the persons present, including the VP. Harish was well versed with the formal pleasantries due to the training he had received. After the introduction he rushed to show the presentation of the product features. He was trying to cover all the slides as he had lost a substantial amount of time. Harish carefully avoided any questions by announcing beforehand that he was short of time. Lastly, the VP had to leave to attend some other meeting. Harish presented all persons attending, with a token. He thanked everybody and closed the presentation.

Questions:

1. Was it an effective presentation?
2. Was Harish's strategy of not allowing others to speak right?
3. Was the presentation properly planned?

Case Study II

Nalini was presenting her market research findings to her MBA class in which the Dean was also invited. She had prepared the slide on an OHP. There were four members in the team and they helped her to prepare the presentation. Nalini being the team leader had to present the findings. She was a bit nervous and tried to cover it up with a chewing gum in her mouth. They had lot of statistical details as back-up material and fifty slides right from objective to conclusion. All the team members were satisfied with the preparation. Each group had fifteen minutes to present.

Nalini started the presentation in English. She was conscious of the Dean's presence and was looking at him while speaking. As she was very particular about her dress and looks, she became very conscious about it. When one of the teachers put up a question, Nalini lost track and did not have the right answer. She got more nervous and did not get the right words to continue. Rajesh, a team member had to come to her rescue. He was not fluent in English so he presented in Hindi. The presentation could not be completed in the allotted time and they could only reach the observation table. The Dean allowed five more minutes to sum-up. But without slides, things were not moving in the right direction. Finally it came to an end with a confused audience.

Questions:

1. Where did the preparation go wrong?
2. Was it right on part of Rajesh to present in Hindi?
3. What is your observation regarding the intervention by the teacher?
4. What more could have been done to make the presentation more effective?

Exercise 1
Evaluation of Effective Speaking

Name of the person: *Topic:*

(A group of three or four persons (preferably friends) can take the chairs of evaluator and rate the person on the following points.)

- **Taking position**
- **Started speaking**
    a) Before taking the position on the dais.
    b) After taking the position.
    c) Speaking even when he is moving.
- **Facing the audience:**
    a) In front of the people.
    b) On the left side of the audience.
    c) On the right side of the audience.

- **Posture while addressing:**
  a) Feet are firm on the ground.
  b) Left foot on the right foot.
  c) Left foot out.
  d) Right foot out.
  e) Both the feet separated by a gap of 6" to 8" apart.
  f) Keep shifting the posture every now and then.
- **Body weight**
  a) On the left foot.
  b) On the right foot.
  c) Equally on both feet.
  d) Keep shifting from one to another.
- **Eye contact**
  a) Looking at people.
  b) Trying to avoid eye contact.
  c) Looking only to one side of the group.
  d) Trying to shift the gaze up and down.
- **Facial expressions**
  a) Pleasant and smiling.
  b) Tense and a stern straight look.
  c) Blank and does not seem confident.
- **Position of hands**
  a) In the pockets.
  b) One hand in the pocket and the other explaining things.
  c) Hanging on the side.
  d) Crossed over the chest.
  e) In front or behind the back.
- **Use of hands** during address
  a) Used to explain.
  b) Adjust clothes, tie, belt, and spectacles.

c) Scratch nose, head, ears etc.
- **Confidence level**
   a) High in confidence.
   b) Low in confidence.
- **Contents of the address**
   a) Well structured and starts with an introduction.
   b) Informative and knowledge based.
   c) Interesting, but not related to the topic.
- **Medium of communication**
   a) English.
   b) Hindi or some regional language.
   c) English mixed with some regional language/Hindi.
- **Command over language and delivery**
   a) Good and fluent.
   b) Average with few stoppages.
   c) Poor with stammering and lot of gaps.
- **Expression**
   a) Clear.
   b) Not clear.
- **Volume and pace of diction**
   a) Ok, with right pace.
   b) Low volume but fast pace.
   c) Very low and slow.
- **Mannerism**
   a) Clearing of throat.
   b) Smacking of lips.
   c) Frequent use of the words/lines 'you see', 'I mean', 'OK'.
   d) Breaks such as 'Anh' and 'Unh'.

If you have got your report card you must check if you have done everything correct. You must not speak before you come on the dais and look in all directions while you speak. The weight should be on both the legs with 6" to 8" gap between your feet. The hands should preferably be on your side. Try to structure the contents and use only one language as you speak. Have a clear and moderate volume so that it is not necessary for others to stop you. All poor mannerisms, as suggested, should be avoided. Regular practice can make you a perfect speaker.

THE ART OF ATTENDING PHONE CALLS

By all means the vital link between you and the people far off, not physically present, is the telephone. Technology has changed several facets of office life, but has not affected the importance of the telephone in the process of communication. A professional who is competent in the use of telephone is a more effective person. Behavioural scientists have identified three very important aspects of effective telephone conversation—the voice, initial opening remarks and telephone decency.

Some basic tips to effectively attend calls are listed below:

- **Make plans to call.** Determine why you are making the call. The caller must be clear of what his opening sentence will be. Many a time someone reminds you that you were supposed to call someone, and in a hurry you call him up but miss

the main topic or issue you wanted to tell him. At some other time you may not be very sure what the opening remarks should be. Give a minute to think before talking to someone important. Never show your hurry in dialling the number.
- **Have a pen and paper ready to take down important information.** When we are talking to someone we may get some vital information which we would like to keep as a record for future reference. It may be very casual information when you are talking, but such information proves vital on a later date.
- **Which person to talk to in the company.** The person should preferably be known. Knowing his name, temperament and liking can be an added advantage. The person we talk to should be relevant. We must reach the concerned person before starting transaction otherwise you may need to repeat the same things over and over again.
- **The conversation should be formal or informal** depending upon the person you are talking to.
- **Confidently ask what you want.** It is difficult to say no to a difficult caller. There is however a difference between confidence and harshness. You have to be polite and confident. The confidence in your call will impress others, not harshness.
- **Never keep hanging on the phone after necessary talk.** Short is sweet and fruitful. You should not keep telling something or the other that can dilute the importance of your main message.

- **Give due importance to the priority of the other person even on the phone.** As we need to hear the other person's view before imposing our own in a face to face conversation, we must allow others to speak on the phone as well. Always remember that an individual's own thoughts are very dear to him.
- **Be Polite.** Even if the person at the other end is adamant to talk to you or rejecting your call, he is not rejecting you or your thoughts. The art is to request for a call some other time.
- **Timing of the call** is very important. Odd hours should be avoided. When calling a person who is generally very busy, try to find some other information like his routine and at what time he prefers to attend calls. Talking to a person who is not in a good frame of mind will not help you to fulfil your objective of calling.
- **Never ask your secretary or spouse to lie that you are not there** when you are. People can easily make out such lies and that is more harmful to the relationship. Just politely ask the caller to call some other time.
- **Do not talk loudly over the phone as it disturbs those around.** We forget the importance of a peaceful working environment and the need for privacy when we are talking. The telephone conversation may be of great interest to you, but others may be cursing you as your decibel level may interfere with their working.
- **Do not smoke while making calls.**

Case Study I

Amitabh, a sales executive in a FMCG, was required to talk to the CEO of a large retailer chain in the city for the promotion of few of the latest products of the company in the retailer chain outlets. For the last two days he had attempted several times to contact him over the phone to get an appointment, but with very little result. Finally he thought of trying something new. He called the office of the CEO just five minutes after it opened. He got the secretary on the line and started explaining to her in detail why the meeting was important. The secretary said she could not keep the phone busy for so long and disconnected. Amitabh went to his Manager to relate this incident.

The Manager, Mr. Juneja, was a seasoned salesman. He enquired who the secretary was and what the routine of the CEO is. What are his likes? As per information available the CEO did not attend any important meetings between 1:00 and 1:30. Juneja called the secretary and started the conversation with, "Hello Ms Jolly. How do you do?" The response was fantastic. He was connected to the CEO within a few seconds and he started by congratulating him for getting elected as the President of the local golf club. Now coming to the business agenda, he requested a small personal favour. The CEO agreed to it and the conversation ended with a promise of their meeting in the near future.

Questions:

1. Where did Amitabh falter?
2. Was it appropriate to address Ms Jolly by her name?

3. Why did Juneja succeed while Amitabh could not?
4. Was talking to the CEO indirectly more effective?

ART OF NEGOTIATION

Whatever you do and whenever you interact with people you are required to negotiate whether it is a business negotiation, a negotiation for development of the community with the local elected member or the negotiation between the parents of prospective bride and bridegroom. We simply cannot ignore the requirement of good negotiation skills. In certain fields of work this skill can make or break your career. If you are a sales professional you must learn this art thoroughly to succeed and cherish the dream of maximising your sales volume through effective negotiation.

We must prepare ourselves well before we take up the position on the negotiation table. The objective for negotiation must be very clear. You are not there to argue or prove your superiority of knowledge, but to settle an issue (where there is a possibility of both having different viewpoints). We are required to attend a negotiation with a preconceived notion and knowing what side we are on. The basic homework required to be done are as under:

1. **Know your opponent:** You must have sufficient information about the person at the other end of the table and the organisation he is representing. You may

find out the strength and weakness of the individual including his temperament. The other important aspect, which can come in handy at the time of negotiation, is the history, capability and resources of the opponent.

2. **Know yourself**: When you arrive at the negotiation table you must have with you the analysis and information about yourself as well as your organisation. Your SWOT analysis (strength, weakness, opportunity, threat) will help you to focus on your strengths and correct your weaknesses.

3. **Possible settlement scenario**: You must be aware of the possible settlement scenario and in what way would it have an impact on you and your organisation. Knowledge of the possible outcome prevents you from the shock of it.

4. **Determine your strategy and limits ahead of time:** When you are at the negotiation table the direction of talks will never be in your control unless you have identified the strategy and the limits of your settlement. Your self-limiting switch must operate when it comes to crossing the set values.

5. **Review:** Each negotiation must be reviewed later to gain knowledge for the next negotiation. What needs to be learnt from such reviews is the area where one lacks and needs to improve. There are certain strong points of the opponent that also should be a lesson for the next negotiation and must be kept in mind.

During a negotiation the interests of the parties involved may clash giving rise to a situation of conflict.

Handling of conflict situation is an important aspect. Tensions must be avoided and it is better not to fool yourself about your temperament. Try to work on your capability to handle conflicts.

Case Study I

Mr Malkani, a successful Indian businessman in his fifties, was heading a group of Indian entertainment electronics company in Mumbai. The company had started in 1981 with Mr Malkani as a very successful TV manufacturer. He then joined hands with a famous Japanese MNC with only a minority stake. In 1989, when the government allowed joint ventures to promote international quality in Indian market, the marriage of convenience proved short-lived as the MNC partner started dominating Mr Malkani with its financial strength.

The Indian partner was being used for the local contacts and marketing, but they were slowly and surely being isolated in the production process and the operational aspects. Mr Malkani was getting suffocated in the situation. Finally, after consulting his friends and well-wishers, Malkani decided to sell his stakes in the company to the overseas partner.

The meeting was fixed in the presence of the financial advisers from both sides for the proposed selling of the shares of Malkani to the Japanese partner. The MNC consultants had done their homework well. They knew that Malkani was not comfortably placed, as far his financial position was concerned. He had received a notice from the income tax department for his default just the week before. They had done a complete study of the areas of strength that Malkani exercised in other industries. The MNC also pushed the price of the other industry in which Malkani was a player. Whereas, Malkani thought that as the Japanese executives did not understand and speak English they would not be able to negotiate well. But it was not true. The financial strength and the limit till which they should stretch were all well planned in the case of the Japanese side.

The meeting commenced at 11:00 a.m. The Japanese delegation was cool with a very professional approach. Mr Akito, Director (Finance) of the company, was heading the team. He came from his seat to receive Malkani and his team. He ensured a cordial business environment and avoided any ill feelings before they talked business. As this was his first visit to India he gifted every member of the Indian team with a gold-plated watch. The meeting started with the opening remarks from the Japanese team leader. The proceedings went on smoothly and the Japanese team never allowed things to go out of control.

Mr Malkani was deliberating most of the time about the price of the factory land, which was only 2.8 per cent of the total cost of sale, but he was emotionally attached with it and was talking in length. The Japanese team allowed bargaining up to 20 lakhs more than what they thought should have been the price for the land. Malkani was happy to get the price that he thought was good. For the price of the shares Malkani agreed within a few minutes to a price lower than what the Japanese thought would be the price to close the sale. The negotiation ended much in favour of the Japanese as they could close the deal at 38 crores, 8 crores less than the figure they had in mind. The meeting ended with a formal signing of the agreement to sell between both the parties.

Questions:

1. Did the negotiation go well for Malkani? If not, why?
2. What made the Japanese successful in clinching the deal?
3. If you are the consultant for Malkani, what are your suggestions for him?

ART OF FACING INTERVIEWS

The most commonly used tool for the selection process is the personal interview. An interview is a conversation with a purpose between two persons or groups of persons. They are done not only for the purpose of recruitment or selection for a post, but also to gather information from someone important.

Even though it is a two-way traffic, it is mostly seen that the employer is the one who asks questions and the interviewee is supposed to reply. Different purposes of a personal interview are—to rate a candidate for his physical appearance, educational achievement and qualification, level of intelligence, background, interests and aptitude. There are different types of interviews, like:

1. **Informal interview**: This is the type of interview that is conducted in an informal setting. The interview can be held at the residence of the Managing Director for

the post of a legal consultant. Similarly, many senior level job assignments are finalised during dinner at some hotel or restaurant.
2. **Formal interview:** This is the interview that is conducted most commonly for recruitment of personnel. In such interviews the candidate is called for an interview at a particular location and time. The candidate is required to answer questions asked, based on the outcome of which he is rated for selection.
3. **Patterned interview:** To maintain a uniform approach there are few interviews where a set pattern of questions are asked. In such patterned interviews the choice of person conducting the interview is restricted and the selection criteria is also limited within a set frame.
4. **Non-direct interview:** The objective of an interview is to select a candidate for a particular post, but if you have a specific job-related area for asking questions, chances are that you may not get a proper feedback. Therefore, instead of asking questions directly pertaining to the job it is better to ask some indirect questions.
5. **Depth Interview:** In such an interview, questions are based upon a specific area of the interviewee's interest. In a depth interview the person has to answer in detail. The academic competence and knowledge is tested thoroughly in such type of interviews.
6. **Stress Interview:** For the selection of supervisory and executive positions, it is of equal importance to judge the suitability of individual competence based on

stress endurance along with knowledge and intelligence. Therefore a candidate is required to appear for the stress interview. In such an interview a person is required to respond to a stress situation and the assessment is done on the basis of his response.
7. **Group Interview:** When we are required to perform a task in a group, the selection is done in a group interview and the candidate along with a group is asked to solve a particular problem. The performance and behaviour is, however, assessed and rated individually.
8. **Panel Interview:** For a senior level position selection, a panel of experts select the candidate.

Personality and behavioural traits are very important for performing well in interviews. Interviews, at times, become a hurdle between success and failure for persons just out of college. You have to present your competence for a particular post or job within a short period of fifteen to forty-five minutes. The candidate is assessed for his behaviour, mannerism, attitude, IQ, stress enduring capability, general awareness, knowledge of the subjects studied and mental frame of mind to take up the position for which he has applied. For a young student it is important that he prepares well for crossing this hurdle. He must be ready for the competitive written examinations as well as for the face-to-face interview.

Listed below are a few interview do nots and usual reasons for failure in interviews that every candidate should keep in mind:

1. The candidate should not lack self-confidence or appear shaky.
2. The *hello-effect* of the candidate should be impressive to the interviewing board.
3. Poor communication skills are an absolute put-off.
4. Body language must not reflect negativity.
5. The candidate must not lack the relevant subject knowledge.
6. There is a difference between self-confidence and over-confidence. Even if the expectation level of the candidate is high, he should not exhibit arrogance.
7. The candidate's background and family history are important.
8. The candidate must have a reasonable amount of knowledge about the company and the industry in which he has applied for employment.
9. The candidate must not be improperly dressed or lack a sense of hygiene.
10. If the interview board is harsh, the candidate must not lose his or her cool during the interview.
11. The candidate must give a focused reply.
12. Also, at times, the number of candidates is very large and board members are unable to give sufficient time to each candidate for answering. Thus, answers should be as precise as possible.

Mostly these are the twelve reasons for poor performance of a candidate, but there may be some other reasons that do not need any mention such as a biased board and other factors to influence the selection process.

Follow the simple rules listed below and perform much better in interviews:

Rule I—Behave as you are: A person facing an interview is generally nervous and does not behave as his or her normal self. He tries to follow the set guidelines that he has been told and in the process becomes very stiff and unnatural. Do not act, be yourself.

Rule II—Reach the interview site well before time: It is seen that people reach the interview venue just before the interview commences. The early arrival at the interview venue will give you time to understand the office culture, the local etiquette and the expectation of the office and a chance to adapt to the particular environment. Reaching in advance also gives you the time to make yourself comfortable and more presentable by giving you time to freshen up. The settling time will help you to handle a difficult situation properly.

Rule III—Try to know the company: If you are appearing for an interview, the interview board expects you to know what the company is doing and what are the industry norms the company is in. Prepare from all sources such as the Internet, company brochure and other sources, if any. Try to find out the company's area of operation and expansion/diversification plans for which they are recruiting people. The mission and vision, and USP (unique selling proposition) of the company concerned can help you to frame your answers as desired by them.

Rule IV—Be focused: The purpose of your appearing for the interview is that you are looking for a job. The questions asked by the board will at times derail your prepared answers and will take you to a different direction. The derailment will compel you to lose sight and answer the way you never planned to. Try to be focused about your strength areas and the requirements of the company concerned. Try to be as short and straight as possible while dealing with a controversial issue.

Rule V—Anticipate the probable questions: When we are to appear for an interview we do have a clue as to what questions the board will ask. Say, a person has an educational gap of two years mentioned on his CV, the board would like to know what the candidate was doing during that period. Similarly, if a person has indicated trekking as his hobby, he must prepare for answering few questions on it. A housewife applying for a teacher's post will in all probability be asked about her routine for the day. Well-prepared answers for irritating questions will help you fare better in the interview.

Rule VI—Behave as if you are already in the job: When a person applies for the job of a front desk manager, the interview board will like to see him in that pretext and would judge him keeping that person in the mould of a manager. If he starts feeling and behaving like a manager, half the work is done.

Rule VII—Be genuine and honest: Never lie to the board members. It is very easy for them to judge the truth or falsity of any statement or claim. Besides, everyone would like to reward your honesty.

Rule VIII—Never have unnecessary worry for your language: There is no doubt that communication and language are very important aspects of an impressive interview, but if you do not have a good command over the English language do not allow this weakness to dominate your area of strength. Unnecessary worry about your weakness of not knowing the English language well will only adversely affect your performance and morale and will make you shaky. Answer the questions in a composed way and never use very complex words to impress others.

Rule IX—Never answer questions about which you are not sure: If you are honest in saying that you do not know the answer, people will appreciate it more than if you guess something absurd.

Rule X—Wish all members before and after the interview: It has been noticed that many candidates do not feel it necessary to wish the members and many others skip it due to nervousness. It does not give a good first impression of the candidate if he does not wish the board members.

Rule XI—Mind your body language: In the preceding pages we have discussed the importance of body language in effective communication. It is extremely important to mind your body language in an interview as you meticulously plan the words you utter.

NETWORKING—A WINNING PROPOSITION

The present age is the IT age and information is the king. We are in touch with our peers, friends, business associates and other persons in the society. There is a growing need to reach out and expand your relationships through networking. For any successful person in this present age, networking is an important function. What is the networking we are talking about? Like all computers in the Internet are connected in a web, in a human relationship network we must know which person has the solution to our particular problem.

Networking can be defined as 'the ability to meet people, attempt to find out the right contacts and people who matter to you and then to develop an unselfish relationship. The final stage is grooming the relationship and servicing it after proper development.'

The following are the benefits of being in a network and developing contacts:

- It gives you an edge over your peers. With the same capability and competence, persons having better contacts are more successful.
- People decide things based on the group you belong to and the contacts you have, and not only on the numbers they see.
- Networking gives you more exposure and the chance to present your capability.
- Persons who are in a profession like marketing get an advantage of meeting new clientele.

- Vacancies are hardly advertised in papers these days and you need to be well connected and have your network if you would like to get a decent job.
- The best of the talents also need some platform to perform and showcase what you are up to.
- Wide social circles can be a blessing in disguise when you need the helping hand from an unexpected corner.
- Networking can help a potential prospect to get the right opening at the right time.

Few basic rules on how to be connected are listed below:

1. **Enjoy meeting people with natural flair.** If you are shy of meeting people and you do not enjoy meeting someone unknown, this is the time for you to rethink. When you say 'it was nice meeting you', there should be genuine pleasure expressed. We need to develop the ability and quality of enjoying the company of others.
2. **Meet people for everlasting impression and exchange cards.** A relationship in a network has an everlasting impression. Relationships developed during your MBA or any other classes shall be for a lifetime. We meet people after years and have the warmth of the bond of the relationship still intact. In a business relationship we must exchange cards and keep all the cards in a nice cardholder, a digital diary and PC. Update all the relationships you have developed. Never think of these small investments on the network as a wastage of money.

3. **Have a habit of being in touch and appreciate the achievement of others genuinely.** We must know the art of being in touch with the other person even after the first meeting. Subsequent meetings give you an opportunity of knowing other people better. Never contact a person only when you are in need of some help. For a good contact and relationship you must have genuine concern. Selfish way of networking does not work well for anyone.
4. **Send greeting cards on all occasions.** The easiest way of keeping any relationship in a network alive is to send greetings on all occasions such as New Year's Day, important festivals or important personal celebrations like birthdays and marriage anniversaries.
5. **Network with people in your area of interest.** We keep meeting people from all walks of life; it may be good networking for a politician, but certainly not a wise networking choice for a professional. He has to identify persons who are important for his profession. If you are a Doctor there is no point in networking with an Interior Decorator. A successful network can only be through your own professional group.
6. **Create a bond for exchange; give and take.** Any fruitful relationship is based on the equation of give and take. If you are interested in forming a fruitful relationship never expect favours only from the other person. If you need to get the support from the other person always be ready to extend your support too.

7. **Keep your relationship in the network alive with regular servicing.** Personal touch is very vital and important for the survival of any relationship in a network. If you keep on adding new names to your network without spending time and energy at keeping the network intact, you are not following the ground rules properly.
8. **Take help of others if your PR is not good.** If your own assessment is that you do not have the necessary flair for forming good contacts, never hesitate to take help of others. A friend, near and dear ones, or even a professional can provide you with the necessary help.
9. **You need to blow the trumpets of your success and achievements.** If you have done something worth mentioning you must convey the achievement through the network to the people who matter. If you do it and others do not know it, it is not an achievement. Use your network for anything worth mentioning.
10. **Network is a two-way traffic; share the network.** If we get the benefit of a network we must not use it for our good alone; we must share this network. The network can expand only if you allow others to use it.

4

Motivation and Self-Motivation

The process of inducing and inspiring anyone to perform his or her functions more productively and efficiently is known as motivation. It is a catalyst that enhances the performance of an individual. If a person is motivated he will try to put his best effort and complete the task assigned to him. Whereas, a de-motivated person may not be able to perform upto his potential and the job that he could have easily completed in a short span of time will take much longer to finish. In any context money acts as the prime motivating factor. This may be true for a person who does not have sufficient money to meet his basic needs, such as food, clothing and shelter. But once he has all his existential needs fulfilled, he may be motivated by some other factors.

Example: A Government employee in a corporation office gets his salary on the very first day. As perks he also gets a comfortable life with job-security, but does he perform his duty when you approach him for a birth certificate, which he is supposed to issue within a few hours? It takes him months to issue that. The reason is that he is not motivated to perform with speed.

When we ask someone to do a certain job, we must identify his motivating factor. Different persons have different motivational needs. Some are motivated by money, others by emotion, and still others by security and, at the same time, there are those who are motivated by recognition and self-esteem. We may be successful in inspiring someone if we can analyse the personal motivational needs of the person.

A person may not have the same motivational needs throughout his life; they change with the growth of the person. The same person at different stages of life has different needs. For a case study try and recall what was the motivating factor for you, three years, six years and nine years back. You will find that it does not remain the same at different stages of life. Some motivating factors are on high priority throughout the lives of successful people and they act as the driving force.

Amit's case study is shown to help you analyse the motivating factors at different ages in his life. Based on it we know that there are different motivating factors for different stages in our life. At the same time, different people are motivated by different motivating factors.

The great behavioural scientist **Maslow** has evolved the five stage motivational needs of a person. The lowest needs of a person are the physiological needs. He likes to

> It is very easy to motivate a one-year-old baby Amit with a lovely toy.
>
> The five-year-old child Amit can be motivated with a chocolate.
>
> Twelve-year-old boy Amit has changed, he has different needs and can be motivated to perform well with a promise of a new cricket bat.
>
> Fifteen year-old Amit is more fascinated by a new cycle. He is ready to do anything if he is promised a new cycle.
>
> Twenty-two-old year Amit is keen to get a nice job and a lovely girlfriend to enjoy life. He is ready to do anything for his job.
>
> Thirty-year-old Amit is well employed, earns well and drives a car. His need is to marry a beautiful girl and gaining stability is his priority.
>
> At fifty Amit has achieved all he wanted and has earned enough. Now he is keen to get respect and recognition in his career. That is what inspires him most.
>
> Amit, the father, at his last stage in his life has his son's career highest on his priority list.

meet his basic needs such as food, clothing etc. **Herzberg,** another famous behavioural scientist, further identified these basic needs. He called these basic human needs the hygiene factor. On the layer above the basic needs a person may look for other needs such as friendship and security. As he is confident of getting it, he may not find it motivating enough to perform better. He will look for other

Personality Development

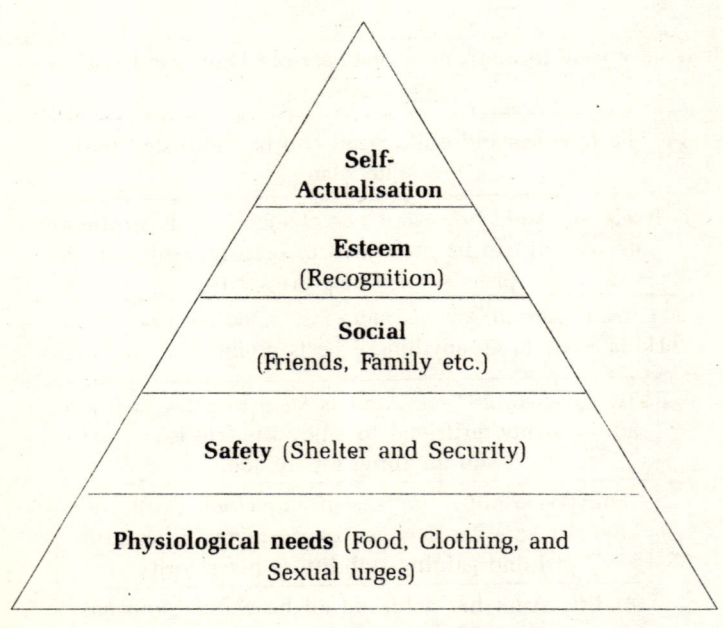

Maslow's Hierarchy of Motivational Needs

motivational needs such as a cordial family, but then he may like to have recognition in the society to which he belongs.

Most people are motivated by external factors and like to achieve greater and greater success with time. But the real achiever is one who inspires himself to achieve the targets that he has set.

Hygiene and Motivators

The great behavioural scientist, Herzberg, has identified the reason for non-performance of highly paid employees of a company. He says that job-satisfaction and motivation are the two dimensions that influence the productivity of an employee. Research shows that in spite of a very good salary, good working conditions, job-security, physical facilities, and good human relationships, the performance of employees is not up to the expected level. Factors such as recognition of work done, status, opportunity for growth, nature of work, responsibility and challenges of work have an integral role to play in motivating people to perform.

Hygiene factors are essential for people to work, but motivational factors play an important role in helping people work more and better. There may be various ways of getting better motivational environment in the company, but the dimensions mentioned below help create conditions where the executives and workers can perform better:

- **Ensure that the executive's time and energy are not wasted on petty things.** *Example*: In a metropolitan city, government officials are paid a poor salary and are not provided with any accommodation near the office. Conveyance is a problem as most of them travel from far off places. Therefore their motivation level is low and that is reflected in the service they provide to the people.
- **Climate of encouraging new ideas and thoughts.** Most Indian companies do not allow any new thoughts or ideas to surface. The ideas of the lower level and younger generation of executives, if given a chance, may prove to be beneficial to the company as well as highly motivating for the young

executive. A team may be allowed to work independently till the time the need for the manager's intervention is felt.

- **Encourage healthy competition and recognise good work.** It is true, companies that give due recognition to its talented executives for their extraordinary efforts do well. In government organisations, where career growth depends on the seniority of a person and the performance and effort is not taken into consideration, the motivation level of personnel who work hard is not high.
- **Show yourself as an example.** If the leader himself is de-motivated he can never expect the team to be motivated. *Example*: If a general in the army accepts defeat, he will present a poor example for other soldiers and the army is bound to lose.
- **Try to create an environment of approach and problem solving.** There are many executives who do not want to face any problems, they would like to avoid anything irritating. This creates an atmosphere of mistrust and de-motivation. Whereas, executives who are willing to solve the problems of others as well as their own create an atmosphere where people will take on their responsibility.
- **Provide for the counselling and guidance of the workers under you.** If you provide counselling to the workers under you when they need it, the motivation level will go up as the trust and faith on the management will increase with such a gesture. Managers who go out of their way to

extend help during distress can get the support of workers when it is needed most.

OTHER MOTIVATION THEORIES

Vroom's Expectancy Theory: Victor Vroom has propounded the most widely accepted explanation of motivation. His theory is commonly known as the Expectancy Theory. It argues that the strength of a tendency to act in a specific way depends on the strength of an expectation that the act will be followed by a given outcome and on the attractiveness of that outcome to the individual. To make this simple, Expectancy Theory states that an employee can be motivated to perform better when there is a belief that better performance will lead to good performance appraisal and that this shall result in realisation of personal goals in the form of some reward.

Therefore, an employee's motivation = **Valence x Expectancy**.

The theory focuses on three things: efforts and performance relationship, performance and reward relationship, and rewards and personal goal relationship. This leads us to the conclusion that

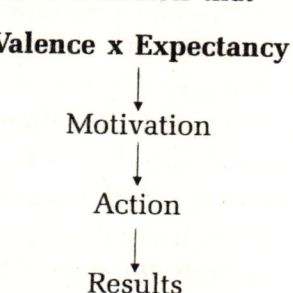

Porter and Lawler Model: Lyman W Porter and Edward E Lawler developed a more comprehensive version of motivation based upon the Expectancy Theory.

Actual performance in a job is primarily determined by the effort spent. But it is also affected by the person's ability to do the job as also by his perception of what the required task is. So performance is the responsible factor that leads to intrinsic as well as extrinsic rewards. These rewards, along with the equity of the individual, lead to satisfaction. Hence, satisfaction of the individual depends upon the fairness of the reward.

Alderfer ERG Theory: Alderfer has tried to rebuild the hierarchy of needs of Maslow into another model named ERG, i.e., Existence – Relatedness – Growth. According to him there are three groups of core needs as mentioned above. The existence group is concerned mainly with providing basic material existence. The second group is the individual's need to maintain interpersonal relationships with other members in the group. The final group is the intrinsic desire to grow and develop personally.

Goal Setting Theory of Edwin: Instead of giving vague tasks to people, specific and pronounced objectives help in achieving them faster. As the clarity is high, goal orientation also avoids any misunderstandings in the work of the employees. The goal setting theory states that when the goals to be achieved are set at a higher standard, then in that case employees are motivated to perform better and put in maximum effort. It revolves around the concept of 'self-efficacy', i.e. an individual's belief that he or she is capable of performing a hard task.

Self-Motivation

Self-motivation is the highest level of motivation. If you have learnt how to motivate yourself, you need not worry about anything. People who can motivate themselves are rare, but they are always better performers in all conditions and environment. People who are influenced and motivated by external factors may not always get the right kind of environment which can motivate them to perform better. Good remuneration is the motivation for performing better, therefore when this reward is not received the individual gets de-motivated. Self-motivated people are, however, not perturbed by small short-term gains.

There are a few *strokes* or *kicks* a person starts getting once he is self-motivated. He who has already achieved some great feat, will try to perform better and better his own record by an inner stroke or kick that he gets with an improved performance. At the age of 29, when he still has many years of cricketing ahead of him, Sachin Tendulkar has already broken the record of scoring the highest number of one-day centuries. The one thing that will motivate him to perform better is self-motivation or the high that he will feel with every subsequent century that he scores.

We all do something or the other for our livelihood. The work we do may be to our liking, but many a time it is not. Performance level is highly improved if we get to do the work we like doing and for which we have the necessary skills. The enhancement of performance in such a case can be depicted by the graphical representation below.

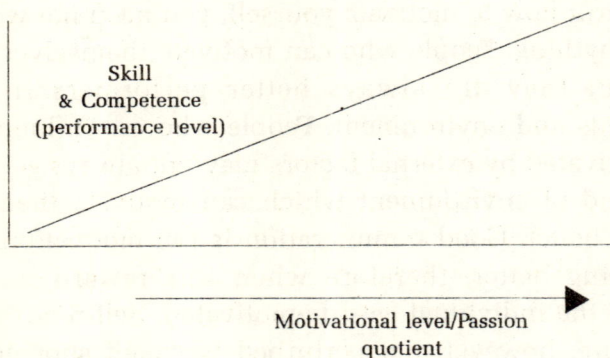

From the above diagram we can infer that we need to enhance the self-motivational level and, at the same time, try to identify the work at which we are competent and which is our strong point.

Case Study I

Muthu has completed his graduation with great difficulty. He belongs to a poor family from Coimbatore. He could not continue his PG in Chennai University, as his father wanted him to take up some job or the other. He was trying desperately to find a job for himself. He appeared in several interviews and written tests but success was eluding him. He was willing to do any kind of job for the sake of it.

His school friend Raghu was working for a textile mill in Coimbatore. He was feeling bad that his good friend Muthu was upset without a job. He suggested to Muthu that he should join the mill as a worker. Muthu never wanted to be a worker in the mill but the financial condition of his family was such that he could not refuse the offer. He went to the line supervisor of the mill. He was selected and joined his duty the very next day. He was happy to start the job. He was very sincere with his assignment and very soon, by virtue of his intelligence, he became very popular in the mill. The floor Manager was highly impressed with his sincerity. One day when the expert mechanic was absent the whole factory came to a standstill due to the failure of a critical machine in the line. The Manager himself tried to repair it but with little success. Muthu went to the Manager and offered his services to repair the machine. Initially the Manager did not allow Muthu to try his luck but once he discussed the issue with the GM, it was decided that there was no harm in trying. Muthu started to repair the motor in the evening shift and after six hours of hard work put the mill back into operation. It was great news for the management. Muthu instantly became a hero for the workers as well as a blue-eyed boy for the Manager.

Muthu was confirmed as a regular worker and was given a cash prize for his performance. Time was running fast but Muthu was not getting the returns for the hard work he used to put in. He was a popular face amongst the workers and as he was educated he started reading the labour laws and learning the Factory Act to give his opinion to the workers when there was any dispute with the management. On the weekend, when there was some problem in the mill, the Manager called Muthu to attend to it. Muthu refused saying that it was not his job.

Next year, the workers union elected Muthu their General Secretary. He was not the same young boy from the village anymore. He started discussing all the labour issues competently with the management. Soon the GM recognised Muthu's strength, who was now the spokesperson for Coimbatore Mill Workers Association. Now he was attending meetings with ministers and the District Administration. The following year, a regional party nominated Muthu as the candidate for the General election. He was elected by a large margin and soon was one of the important MLAs in the ruling party.

Questions:

1. Was Muthu's decision to join politics right?
2. Were the motivational factors for Muthu, as a young worker, sufficient?
3. What are your suggestions to improve motivation for the mill workers?

5

Leadership Qualities and Ways to Influence Others

Leadership is the quality of a person that helps separate the men from the boys. It can transform an ordinary person into an extraordinary person. Leadership quality is a must for any field of life, whether it is a battlefield, playground, business establishment or a college students' association. In the history of mankind there have been few leaders who were gifted with leadership qualities. They were born with it, such as Mahatma Gandhi, JRD Tata, Russi Modi, Napoleon and Abraham Lincoln. But at the same time there are some leaders who developed these qualities with great efforts. Business leaders such as Darbari Seth, J J Irani and Anil Ambani are the people in this category.

We all admire people with great leadership qualities. They command respect from their team members. A good leader needs to be task-oriented, but at the same time he must be a person whom other members of the team can rely upon in the time of crisis. He gives direction, but he always remains a part of that job. Leadership is the process of influencing others to work willingly for a group objective. There may be different styles of leadership such as human relationship style, authoritarian, democratic, *laissez-faire* (no control), employee orientation, consideration and initiating structure styles. It will be too early to say which style is good or bad. Based on the situation, environment and the personality traits of the leader, he can choose the style which suits him best.

There are many leadership theories that were propagated based on some experiment to analyse the leadership style. The first to undertake such studies was **Hawthorne** of USA in 1932. There are more than ten such theories propagated by famous behavioural scientists. Some of them are:

1. **Hawthorne Studies (1932):** This was the first study conducted to find out how leadership styles have an impact on other people's performance. The studies were conducted in an electrical bulb factory and with the conclusion that a change in the attitude of workers towards each other and their feeling of togetherness can help increase productivity. The experiment caused an improvement in the importance of workers thereby increasing production. The study suggests that a good leader does take care of this aspect in his leadership.

Leadership Qualities and Ways to Influence Others 103

2. **McGregor, Theory X and Y (1960):** The theory says that there are two categories of leaders having different viewpoints about their subordinates. One group (say X) who believes that most people dislike work and will try to avoid it as soon as they get a chance. Only a small group of people are responsible and like to take initiative. Whereas the other group (say Y) are those who believe that people are responsible and will work hard if their personal needs are satisfied. In Theory Y there is hardly any difference between leader and follower.
3. **Lippit and White, IOWA Leadership Studies (1939):** In this study the leaders are categorised into three categories namely, autocratic, democratic and *laissez-faire* (no control).
4. **Likert, Michigan Studies on Leadership Style (1961):** The studies conducted in the Michigan Survey Research Center have identified two major categories of leaders—one that is employee-oriented and the other that is productivity-oriented. We may find that there can be a judicious mixture of both the leadership styles for an effective leadership.
5. **Stodgil, Ohio State Studies on Leadership Style (1957):** The studies were based on a detailed questionnaire to find out the behavioural description of a leader. Two major dimensions emerged from the studies, one was 'Consideration—relationship and mutual respect for subordinates, trust, feeling, warmth etc.' and the other was 'Initiating the structure—defining role, goal attainment of subordinate'.

6. **Kelly, Trait Theory of Leadership Style and Leadership (1974):** This is one of the very commonly accepted theories of leadership. In this theory, Kelly tried to classify the personal traits of a successful leader. These traits are divided in to six major categories, namely, physical characteristics, background, intelligence, personality (aggressive, alertness, dominance etc.), task oriented and social characteristics. Many behavioural scientists take these traits as the indicators for successful leaders.
7. **Hollander and Julian, Group and Exchange Theory of Leadership (1969):** In this theory the group dynamics is the basis for all the major leadership success. If in the group there is a positive exchange between the leaders and followers, the group goals can be achieved easily.
8. **Bandura, Social Learning Theory of Leadership (1977):** In this theory, leaders and subordinates have a negotiable and interactive relationship.
9. **House, Path Goal Theory of Leadership (1971):** This theory says that the leader is to smoothen the hurdles in the path of achieving the goal. Leader must be the person who has ability to persuade others to get the work done.
10. **Blake and Mouton, Managerial Grid Theory (1978):** This theory is based on a perpetual mapping of the leader on two dimensions in a scale of 0-9; the two dimensions are task oriented and person oriented. If a leader is placed at 9,1, he is primarily concerned about the task, whereas if a leader placed at 1,9, he is primarily concerned with people.

Types of Powers Enjoyed by a Leader

Legitimate power is the power that comes to the leader from the authority in the organisation. For example, the Chairman of a company has the power to recruit a new manager to improve the PR of the company. The power to recruit is a legitimate power of the Chairman.

Expert power is the power of knowledge and skill. When a leader is a skillful software professional, he would get the power to dictate terms in a software company. His decisions will be final. For example, a good surgeon has full powers to run the OT as per his choice as he has the expertise and only he can run the show.

Charismatic power: This is the power of attraction or devotion; people start admiring the leader. The great Indian leader, Indira Gandhi, had the charisma to attract large Indian masses. She was loved by all for her presence and enigmatic personality.

Reward power: This is the present and potential ability of the leader to reward good and worthy behaviour and performance. Any leader who can reward a good work done by his subordinate will enjoy the power of rewarding. For example, a cricket captain who can select a player for his final eleven will exercise the power of reward in motivating young players to perform better.

Coercive power: This is the ability to threaten or punish. The worst of all the powers to exercise control on the behaviour of another person is coercive power. For example, a mafia don commands the power to punish the local businessman, as the local businessman fears the unlawful muscle power of the don.

Difference between Authority and Power

The leadership process deals with different ways of influencing others. It is important for us to know power and authority differ. Authority is the right to command and extract obedience from others, it generally comes with the post or chair you occupy. It comes from the organisation you belong to and has very little to do with the individual concerned. Authority is the ability vested on a person to exercise control on the behaviour of other persons whereas the leadership of a person can influence others and control them. The authority does bring in with it some of the legitimate powers, but there are other powers that depend very much on the style of leadership.

The Major Attributes of Leadership

There are only two types of people in this world—a **leader** and a **follower**. Yes, all people want to become leaders, but there will be only one who will lead a bunch of followers. Earlier people used to say that a leader is born and cannot be trained, but such concepts have considerably changed in the recent past. A leader who may have reached great heights and can motivate people to achieve big goals has very likely been a follower himself at one point of time. Such people become leaders by closely planning, thinking and implementing the basic traits (like the ones mentioned below) which separate a leader from a follower.

1. **Courage:** No leader in this tough world can be thought of without the very basic trait of courage. If you lack the courage to take a calculated risk and lead the team for such an adventure, you will never gain in your life. The courage you show to the team members will motivate and inspire them to work harder to achieve the objective. Subhas Chandra Bose could inspire thousands of Indians on only one basic factor, which was his courage and confidence in his mission. The followers look at their leader as a security ring. The leader's courage should be based on knowledge of self, and of one's occupation. No follower wants to be dominated by a leader who lacks self-confidence and courage.
2. **Self-control:** The man who has no control on himself can never control others. Set an example for others. Self-control is essential to show people what is expected of them.
3. **A keen sense of justice and fairness:** If you are not fair to all your followers, biased towards some of the handpicked loyal and prefer to be surrounded by those people only, there is every possibility that your followers will not have any respect for you as a leader. No leader can command and retain the respect of followers if he is unfair and has no sense of justice. The large business houses such as Enron in USA could not sustain its prime position as people had little faith in the fairness of the leader.
4. **Definiteness of plans:** Never be like a rudderless ship. Have a definite plan of action. The followers would

like to see you as the one who can steer their ship even in stormy weather. If you do not have the correct road map and plan how can you think of reaching the goal that you have set and which may not be visible to your followers?

5. **The habit of doing more than being paid for:** As a leader you are the role model for others and whatever they see in their leader they will follow suit. If a leader is not putting his best efforts in his work, none of his followers will put in his best.

6. **A pleasing personality:** No leader is expected to be a rustic and rude person. People see the leader as their representative to the outside world. A corporate Chairman and CEO who is representing an international IT company must have a pleasing personality.

7. **Sympathy and understanding:** The people under you regard you as their guardian and expect your empathy just like a father in the joint family. The interest of the father has to take the back-seat if he desires his son to perform better.

8. **Mastery of details:** The followers look up at their leader for guidance and direction towards the goal. Therefore you are required to know the details of the work to be a true leader.

9. **Willingness to assume full responsibility:** A leader is required to take up the responsibility for any mistakes of the subordinates. The leader should be ready to take more responsibility for the growth.

10. **Co-operation:** A leader is a leader as he is leading a

team. If there is no team spirit there is a possibility that his authority and his effectiveness will be questioned. The creation of a conducive and co-operative environment is a must for an effective leadership.

Causes for Major Leadership Failures:
- Inability to organise details.
- Unwillingness to provide service.
- Fear of competition from followers.
- Lack of imagination.
- Selfishness.
- Disloyalty.
- Emphasis of the authority. A good leader must lead by encouraging.
- Emphasis of title. Generally people who lay more emphasis on their status and title, care very little for their followers.

Principles of Influencing Others

In a nutshell, we would like to list few of the behavioural qualities a person should have. A leader's job is to change people's attitude and behaviour. A famous behavioural scientist suggested a guideline that is still valid. These are to be practised by those who aspire to become leaders of a group.
1. The relationship must begin with genuine praise and honest appreciation.
2. Never pinpoint mistakes directly.
3. Start by stating your own mistakes if you want to criticise others.

4. Direct orders may not be a welcome thing. Rather ask questions.
5. Other person must never be pushed to the wall.
6. Never be at a loss of words for praise of any improvement.
7. Encourage others to live up to a fine reputation.
8. Others must happily accept your suggestion.

Case Study I

Gopalan was the new Administrative Officer of the Hotel Continental, a five-star hotel famous for its grandeur. The new officer was trying to assess the situation and the performance of each team member. There was a housekeeping team of eleven cleaners and two supervisors in the group. They were to look after the entire housekeeping job of the hotel. There was one person in the housekeeping team named Venu who was very calm and always preferred to be alone. Others informed that he was not a good worker and always delayed the work. The supervisor Mathew was critical of his behaviour too.

Gopalan called Venu to his room and asked him to speak for himself. Venu said that he was not very happy with the behaviour of his colleagues and was particularly distressed due to the harsh words used by Mathew. He also informed Gopalan that when he wanted a week's leave to attend to his ailing mother, Mathew denied it saying that it was the peak season.

Gopalan took the case of Venu as the first task of his new assignment. He asked him to report to him the next day. He changed Venu's assignment from housekeeping of the kitchen to the front desk and main lobby (supposedly an important assignment). Venu seemed happy with the change. He went to lunch break at 2.30 on that first day, whereas the regular time was 1 pm. When Gopalan went for a round at 3 pm, he found Venu's colleague pulling Venu for not doing a nice cleaning. Gopalan saw that the job was not of high standard, but he appreciated him for his hard work and sincerity. Time went by fast and, with the encouragement from the new Manager, Venu did improve his punctuality and quality of housekeeping. The transformation was commendable. The management recognised the efforts and recommended a cash prize for Venu.

Questions:

1. What are the reasons for Venu's poor performance?
2. How did his peers' behaviour affect his performance?
3. Do you think Mathew was handling him correctly?
4. What is the main reason for the transformation in Venu?

Case Study II

The National Steel Company is the leading manufacturer of steel in private sector. The company was a pioneer in its field and was a profitable company since its inception by the legendary industrialist Manish Gupta. The company was on a decline since the last few years because the government had liberalised the import of steel from south Asian countries. The company engaged the leading international consultant Arthur Andersen to study the state of affairs in the company.

The consultant, after a detailed study, recommended few things including large scale restructuring and reduction of manpower through VRS. The twelve layers of executives must be flattened to four layers and the MBO (management by objective) style should be adopted with few key responsible persons. Manoj Agarwal, 36, was working in the company as Sr Manager (Marketing) since the last seventeen years. He had always been a lovable boss and a peoples' Manager. But with the changing time, the attitude of the management changed drastically. They always felt Agarwal was more a relationship-oriented leader than the task-oriented type.

Agarwal wanted to change his style. He started behaving tougher with his juniors. The situation did not change for good; rather it deteriorated further as the juniors started doubting his intentions. He was under tremendous pressure of losing his job. He met a counsellor who advised him to pursue the interest of the company above his need of relationship. Manoj, after a few days, met his marketing chief and appraised him of the difficulty in the new work culture. The chief said that it is the organisational goals that are above all other individual goals, therefore the team must strive for the organisational goal of working together and fighting the recession period. The chief also suggested that in such a flattened organisation the role of the leader and follower change frequently and have to be flexible and that Manoj must switch over his role as per the job requirement.

Questions:

1. What is your opinion about the difficulty being faced by a leader like Manoj?
2. Is the effort of change and transformation on part of Agarwal sufficient?
3. Was the Chief right in saying that a flat organisation has more flexibility than the conventional one?

Management Information System (MIS)

In this age of information all decisions are taken by top-level management based on the data and information available to them. The data collection, processing, analysis and decision support is greatly improved with better hardware available to today's manager. But still there is plenty of scope for improvement in the managerial information system. MIS refers to the system by which information is collected, processed and presented to the management. Accurate and proper information can lead to better decisions. The important aspect of effectiveness of any manager or an executive is his ability to take excellent, correct and timely decisions. This can be possible only if the right MIS supports it. The MIS has three major components:

1. Raw data from the field (Input).
2. Processing by the system (Processing).
3. Presenting the report, summaries to the management (Output).

Example: The sales figures collected from all the area

managers for the General Manager (Marketing) is the MIS for the Sales Division of the company.

An effective MIS should be:

1. **Timely:** The importance of any information can be of use only if it reaches the decision-making authority in time. The MIS is relevant if it is timely.

    Example: A company is trying to launch a shampoo in the Indian market. It engaged a market research firm that wanted to do an excellent report on the consumer choice of bottle size, but in doing so they delayed the report by a month. The company launched the product in the meantime. Of course the report was of little use to the management.

2. **Accurate:** If the information presented is not accurate it may lead to a wrong decision, therefore the MIS report must be accurate. Most MIS reports are used to take decisions that have an everlasting effect on the strategies adopted by the company. The decision is dependent on accuracy. Some of the less important decisions taken day-to-day may not be as badly affected even if the accuracy level is low.

    Example: The Managing Director is interested in knowing the annual amount paid as wages to a particular production unit in order to find the fixed cost to the company. Even if the Manager (Finance) gives a figure, which is less than 97 per cent accurate, the figure may be useful for the MD.

3. **Relevant:** There may be plenty of reports with volumes of data available in the office, but when a

particular information is sought the same is not available. Storing of unnecessary information is not going to help the management take any useful decision.

Example: The HR department is maintaining the information of all the employees in a particular mill. The Director (Personnel) of the company, before launching a computer training programme, is interested in knowing how many of them are graduates. The personnel manager was unable to find the relevant information from the HR data.

MIS has different **requirements** for different levels of management in the organisation. The top level is concerned about the external environment of the business and is expected to get all the relevant information from the external factors. The government policy, the competitors and information about inputs are critical for the survival and growth.

The middle level manager has to utilise the resources at his disposal properly. Therefore, he has to get all the inventory level, production planning and marketing information relevant to him in time so that any decision to change the planned schedule can be taken well in time.

The lower level business executives have to take decisions based on the day-to-day information collected. They are not bothered about the previous records and long-term future of the company. The data and inputs from market sales figures can give him the deviation of sales from the target as per forecasted figures.

6

Influence of Friends on Your Personality

Friends have tremendous influence on your actions and behaviour. The great poet Tulsidas has very correctly said that to improve your personality you need to leave the company of bad elements. You may say that whatever your friends are doing, you have kept yourself isolated and are not influenced by it. People quote the example of sandalwood, which is not poisoned by the deadly snakes wrapped around it. But it may not be true for you. You will be recognised by the company and people with you and your deeds will be rated by what your friends do.

Most of us accept the offers of our friends, whether good or bad. We do it mostly not to hurt them or risk our friendship. But true friendship is not the one in which your genuine interest is vitiated. We have to find out who are our real friends. You are very fortunate if you have friends who are concerned for your well-being genuinely.

At times friendship is used as a mask to cover the jealousy, animosity or intentions of ditching you when you need a friend most. Friendship is a marvellous relationship, but we must have the wisdom to separate the friends and foes.

'Associate with men of good qualities, if you esteem your own reputation; for it is better to be alone than in bad company.'

— George Washington, First President of USA.

Peer pressure is a great negative influence on our lives. When you are in high school, you start with a few puffs a day as your friend said you shall never be considered a grown-up person if you cannot smoke. Have you ever realised the cost you paid in your life to impress your friends? You must have spent an unaccountable amount smoking and in turn harming the vital parts of your body. Starting as experiments of growing up, these initial bad habits picked up under the influence of friends are carried as legacy of your bad company throughout your life.

When you passed school you went home with a matriculation certificate as well as a certified chain-smoker as a complimentary gift from your peers. You are not earning, so to keep the habit going you face all sorts of difficulty to get the money to buy yourself a smoke. Soon after, in the college hostel, you meet some of your so-called bosom buddies who care for your real growth and want to see you high in position and personality. They will come up with the best way to celebrate or mourn anything – drinking. That is one thing that separates a man from the boys. You cannot ignore their offer as you will be ridiculed and declared unfit for such marvellous company! You start celebrating your high days with them and end up a drunkard. When you are out of college you have acquired a degree for the academics, but your friends have honoured you with being a sporty drinker!

'No one can make you feel inferior without your consent.'

— Eleanor Roosevelt, former First Lady of USA.

Then you reach University. Parents think you are under tremendous pressure due to studies. But, in fact, you are under tremendous pressure to indulge in all sorts of activities other than studies by your so-called friends. They will advise you as if they have seen everything under the sun. They will encourage you not to work hard for your examination as they will suggest fools do it and you can always procure the question papers well in advance. To prove to your friends that you are not a fool you will put studies on a back burner and look for alternate means to score well. You are out from university with a PG degree but also accredited for your lazy attitude. You cannot work hard now as you have left the habit behind. You prepare for being unemployed after such a costly education you acquired with the help of your wonderful friends who were with you all the time.

7

Etiquette and Mannerism

Etiquette is necessary to have an effective and well-groomed personality. Public mannerisms and etiquette should be such that they can create an everlasting impression on the people you meet. We must possess qualities to build a personality that is charming, decent, lovable and welcome wherever we go. Therefore we cannot ignore it. Certain people pick up these habits while still at school, but there are many of us who never had such an opportunity or exposure. The doors are not shut for them also. There is no age, time of the year or period of life when you cannot learn the art of better public mannerisms. We may be well-trained by our parents and teachers who try and instil in us the importance of being well-mannered. Our manners are categorised as good or bad depending on the kind of society we live in. If we are not toilet trained and do not hesitate to pee in the open facing a wall of a public building, it is because we are trained since childhood like that. We have seen all our seniors in the society behaving the same way. Can we do the same thing that we do in the city of Kolkata or Patna in places like London or Frankfurt? Of course not!

Some very poor mannerism often noticed in Indian youth are:

- Biting nails when in stress.
- Picking teeth in public.
- Making slurping sounds while drinking and eating.
- Picking of nose with fingers.
- Spitting in public places.
- Shouting and talking loudly over telephone much to the discomfort of others.
- Crossing the road wherever you feel like.
- Sitting with your back facing someone.
- Sitting on the office table.
- Cutting rude and vulgar jokes in front of lady colleagues.
- Ridiculing someone for his physical limitations and shortcomings.
- Treading on grass in the park.
- Occupying the street in a group while walking on the pavement.
- Jumping queues.
- Not allowing others to complete their sentences.
- Not leaving seats reserved for ladies and disabled persons.
- Smoking at a prohibited place.

- Barging into someone's room without permission.
- Participating in spreading rumours.

The general reason for making us breach the code of civility or forget social courtesies is sidetracked conduct, cultural heritage, and states of morality we follow or simply, eccentricity. If you want to be respected in society, you must also respect society.

One good thing about a human being is the capability to change. An Indian in a few years time can learn French better than a French national or a Britisher who lives in India for years and starts behaving like an Indian. Therefore we can always change our behavioural mannerisms for the better. Any impressive personality whether in India or America has to follow a code of conduct which is applicable not only in a particular state or a country but throughout the globe.

The breeding ground of all good and bad manners is the home. If a young boy has always seen his elders in the family abusing the female members, he will never hesitate in doing that. Many people are in the habit of walking around in shorts or a dress that is not presentable while they are at home. They must have learnt all this from their parents. Of course, all good manners must start at home. If Mr Lal walks across to the balcony of his second-floor flat to spit out a jet of betel juice, why would his teen-aged son bother to throw his Coke can into a bin?

There are many educated people with their children attending good public schools. When they arrive into a movie hall in full family strength, their kids clamber onto the seats and spill popcorn all over while the adults constantly guffaw in the darkness. These are not acceptable in any civilised society. To each person his set of codes, traits and notions of civility is the reference of the mannerism. An Indian would find it discourteous to unwrap a gift as soon as he receives one, while an American would deem it ill-mannered not to open it and express his delight.

The use of toilet and using fingers to eat your meal are some of the common points we generally consider important for behaving nicely in public places. It surely can get sticky in a melting pot. The radicals would beg to differ. Being gallant to women and graceful to men is fine, but why be finicky about how to use the potty or how to handle a fork, they ask. Are not some principles too trivial? If the host removes his jacket at the eating table, must you remove yours too? Must you make sure you do not slouch or look casual while eating?

Ask Judith Martin, who writes the globally syndicated column, 'Miss Manners', and has published several books on etiquette. Says she: 'Even the most apparently trivial etiquette rules are dictated by principles of manners which are related to, and sometimes overlap with moral principles. Respect and dignity, for example, are two big principles of manners from which a lot of etiquette rules are derived'.

But manners are more about considering the feelings of others than just about blending with the best. And it's also about taking responsibility. Have you not heard these sentences when you are using some public services? The poor upkeep of railways is always in question. The government is to take all the blame for the condition of hospitals, public parks and roads. Why are we so unperturbed and participate in these dirty games of blaming others for all the bad things we get? To begin with a better etiquette and responsible behaviour to society, you must think twice next time when you are asking these questions:

- Is not the upkeep of roads the government's job?
- What is the benefit of following rules when none is doing so?
- This country and society is not civilised.
- Where are the public toilets?
- Who the hell follows rules anyway?
- So what if my nephews are raising hell in the neighbourhood? After all, 'boys will be boys'.

If you think the world is your own, you will be more careful of people and their belongings. If you feel like an alien you will behave like one. It just goes to show that the ones exhibiting bad manners and 'I don't care a damn' attitude are the ones who are the real social outcasts while the polished ladies and gentlemen are the people every body gravitates towards.

We must try to avoid the following things in public:

Eating Habits: A gentlemen is identified when he is eating and a lady when she is talking. This is an old saying, but very true at any point of time. Uncouth and bad table manners can send a very sorry message to the people sharing the table with you. Nobody will complain about this, but people do mind such behaviour.

- Take as much as you can eat. Wasting and spilling food is not an accepted behaviour anywhere in the world.
- Slurping, belching while eating in public is considered bad manners. If per chance you have picked up this bad habit, try to discontinue it. Practise eating with a closed mouth and avoid slow eating, it will help you to give up the slurping while eating.
- Hunching over one's food at the table must be avoided, as this is an awkward posture for eating.
- Try not to eat and chew with one's mouth open. The unpleasant sound and scene is repelling for others. This will pose a poor picture of your behaviour.
- Picking one's teeth in public after food is a very common sight after a heavy meal in Indian homes. If it is a must to pick something, you can use a toothpick and must not do it in public.

Public speaking: The art of public speaking was discussed in detail when we were discussing effective communication skills, but as far as etiquettes are concerned we must identify few habits which are not acceptable in any society.

- We must not interrupt someone when he is talking. It is considered highly ill-mannered if you do not allow the other person to complete his sentence.

Public Behaviour

- We must care for the privacy of others and if we are travelling in a public transport, such as a bus or train, we must not talk or laugh loudly to distract others. Talking and laughing loudly in public is not considered good behaviour.
- You are free to listen to the music of your choice, but blaring music from your car or home can be a cause of disturbance to others. Such behaviour must be avoided.
- When we are attending a call, the person at the other end perceives you and your personality based on what you say and how you say it.
- We may dial a wrong number. It is a human error, but not apologising when one dials a wrong number is uncouth.
- We know that it is an art to be a good listener and for successful communication you need to be attentive to what the other person is saying. Not looking at a person when he or she is talking is one thing that can spoil the essence of good communication.

Hygienic Behaviour: By your hygienic habits in public your behaviour will be perceived. We must never ignore the smaller hygiene issues such as:

- The smaller habits make the man what he is. When you are spitting in a public place you are not only allowing others to be affected by the germs in your

mouth, but you also portray a very poor image of yourself. Mend your ways.
- Blowing one's nose in public must be avoided.
- If you are not organised at your home front and are in the habit of littering your house, people will certainly not have a very high opinion about you.
- It is nice to distribute your love to your pet, but a pet is your responsibility and if you are habituated of leaving pet excreta on the pavement you have a scope for improvement in your hygienic behaviour.
- We all need to attend to the call of nature. In civilised society we have identified places for that, easing oneself in public must be avoided. Just imagine a familiar face seeing you doing that in a public place. It can be a cause of great embarrassment and dent your image.

Behaviour on Road: The road is a place where we behave unconsciously and without realising what we are up to. If we can improve our road and traffic behaviour we can improve our public behaviour to a great extent.

- Why do we try to flout traffic signals and jump queues? Does it save some time for us? There answer is no. This is an attitude and poor public mannerism. If you find some one jumping the queue, you immediately perceive him to be arrogant and indisciplined. We must avoid these poor habits.
- Blowing the horn unnecessarily is one aspect in which we Indians are much ahead of any nation in

the world. We keep one hand on the horn and never spare a moment to use it. It is certainly an area we Indians must try to improve.
- We do not respect others and their rights. If we are on the roads or even on a pavement we like walking in a group abreast on the sidewalk. This is certainly avoidable.

Behaviour in a Meeting: When we are in a meeting there are a few basic etiquettes which need to be followed, these are:

- Introducing a friend. It is always bad manners not to introduce someone when they are in a meeting.
- In India, which is a multilingual country, it is highly undesirable to start discussions in a language that is not known to all.
- When there is a large group discussing something, avoid parallel smaller group gossiping.
- Try not to speak when someone else is addressing. If it is an urgent interruption, take permission from the speaker, even if he is a junior colleague of yours.
- Avoid chewing guthka, smoking or eating during a meeting.
- Never shout or talk loudly to impress the gathering or to score a few points.
- Try to stick to the agenda of the meeting.
- Never talk only about you, your company or your own agenda, but allow others also to express their viewpoints if they are invited for the meeting.

- Disregarding RSVPs is a very poor habit and somehow an inbuilt defect of the Indian psyche. Try to mend it as soon as possible as it will stand you in good stead.

Case Study I

Mohanty had to appear for a GD (group discussion) for the campus recruitment for GET, a reputed Iron and Steel company in Eastern India. Mohanty had always secured top slot in the class. He was confident that the company would choose him. The GD was scheduled at eleven in the morning. Rest of the boys arrived fifteen minutes in advance, but Mohanty arrived just at eleven. The recruitment consultant had already intimated about the rules and the time for the GD. Mohanty had to ask the rules again as he could not listen to it in the first instance. Mr Sharma, the consultant, was not happy to repeat it. The first thing he did was to identify a team leader for the GD. He identified Sukanta, a polished and cheerful candidate, as the leader; the topic was 'Impact of MNCs Arrival on Indian Industries'.

Mohanty had always considered himself superior to others in the class. He did not find it comfortable to accept Sukanta as the moderator. When the GD started, he was intervening every now and then. At one point of time when Romesh was expressing his viewpoint, Mohanty lost his temper and virtually started shouting to impress his awareness. The discussion was virtually reduced to words of war between Mohanty and rest of the boys. Finally after the stipulated time, the discussions came to an end.

Mohanty was happy that he could dominate the proceedings. Sukanta remained cool till the end and he summed up the discussion in three lines in clear terms. In the evening the results were declared on the main placement notice board. Mohanty could not believe his eyes when he did not find his name in the list. Sukanta was very much in the list and perhaps was rewarded for his cool moderation.

Questions:

1. What reason do you think is attributable to Sukanta's selection?
2. Why was Mohanty's potential and competence neglected?
3. What is your opinion about time management of Mohanty?
4. What are the other ways to improve the quality of discussion in such a heated environment?

Case Study II

Mr Sharma was travelling in a train; the compartment he was travelling in was a second-class reserved bogey. He had reservation for his family consisting of four members. He was a religious person and a strong believer in God. He was very upset to see that some local travellers occupied the seats booked by him. Mr Sharma was travelling with a lot of luggage. As soon as he entered, there was a big scuffle between Sharma and the daily passengers. The scuffle started becoming physical with a few pushes from each side. The local travellers cooled down when an old person intervened and offered them some other seat. Sharma was no longer in a good mood.

The train crossed many stations and different places. It was hot and humid. Then there were a few moments of tension growing between the two groups again when there was a discussion regarding the policies concerning religion being followed by the Central Government. There were two sets of people from different communities in the compartment. The discussion started as a debate, but the pitch of discussion became harsh and ended in a hot exchange of words from both sides. Once the issue was at its peak, there was a shout from the other end of the compartment, a robber snatched the gold chain of a lady and ran away.

People were consoling the lady telling her that the unfortunate moment was the result of bad luck. The lady was crying as she said it was the only memory of her late mother. The train journey for Sharma's family ended with the entire family soaked in depression of the sorrowful train environment.

Questions:

1. What are the troubles that could have been avoided?
2. Was the area of concern and area of influence for travelling of passengers the same?
3. Why did Sharma lose the opportunity of an enjoyable train journey?
4. Do you think there was any scope of reducing the tension of co-passengers?

Case study III

Tom Williams is a young lad in the first year of a private Medical College in Pune. He belongs to a rich family from Gujarat. His parents have several tea estates in North-eastern India and his father has sent him to Pune only to acquire some qualification. His monthly expenditure is more than the salary of the Dean of the college. He has a Ford Ikon for his personal use. He feels proud to park his car next to the Dean's old Maruti 800. He stays in a luxury flat in a posh locality of the town. With the kind of living standard he has, he has little respect for the teachers in the college.

He is very casual in his approach towards studies. He hardly attends the first class of the day. He is used to wearing casuals and has a very strange kind of hairstyle. Since his arrival in the college this year he has started violating the stringent rules laid down in the college. He says that he does not believe in any rules. He had once gone to the college Welfare Section with the idea of allowing the local fast food owner to start a fun-centre in the campus. His argument was, all work and no play makes Jack a dull boy, a good doctor has to have a pleasing personality and can learn medicine only if he is given a refreshing environment of learning. In a few months of his stay in the college he had a strong following. He was very popular among the girls.

Tom had to appear in the first term exams for which he was under pressure, as he had not devoted sufficient time to studies. He went to his close friend Harish for help, but he too was also not of much help. All the students themselves were nervous, as it was the first exam for them. He went to the Registrar to postpone the exam for a fortnight. The Dean was not willing to shift any dates, as it would be bad for the academic session. Tom called a general meeting of the class in the canteen and they decided to boycott the exams protesting against what they called the inflexible attitude of the Dean.

Ramesh, a sincere student of the class from a middle-class family, did not want to lose a single day for the whims of Tom. He went to the Dean and told him the plans of the students to boycott the exams. The Dean was annoyed with Tom from the very beginning and he rusticated him from the college. But Tom took this as his personal animosity with Ramesh; he made it a point that the class socially boycotted Ramesh. The rift between the two turned violent and college was closed *sine die*.

Questions:

1. Was the discipline in college affected by students like Tom?
2. Was the new concept of fun with studies propagated by Tom right for a country like India?
3. Was it ethically right on the part of Ramesh to inform the Dean of what happened in the college canteen?

8

Sense of Humour

The world is full of sorrows and everyone is facing some problem or the other. If there is some escape from these sorrows, it is the lighter moments in our life when we can forget the moments of our worry, and tension of life. The person who can bring such a relief is always welcome. When we are doing something in which success is far away and we are down with failure we need a break from the gloom and sorrow of not getting what we wanted.

This is the time when we must give a thought to assess which is a better way to lead our life. Is it better to carry with us gloominess to the places we visit, people we meet and make the surrounding gloomy, or take with us a sense of refreshing personality which is symbolic of happiness and positive change? There are a few people you must have met who are living examples of all the sorrow in this world, they are always complaining about everyone including their own self. They will say that they are born with misfortune and are not successful for the simple reason that they have not been granted the fate of a successful man, whereas there are people who will be smiling even when they are undergoing tremendous pain. A humorous person met with an accident and suffered several broken bones and bruises on his face. When his friends went to see him and asked how he was, he replied that he was just fine and laughed wondering how funny he must be looking with the bandages all over his face.

The great Indian Mughal king Akbar was so pleased with the sense of humour of Birbal that he appointed him a Minister in his Cabinet. His sense of humour used to bring in the much-needed relief from the most difficult job of governing such a big and difficult kingdom like India. A sense of humour should be very clearly different from mockery and cheap jokes. You must differentiate between mockery and ridiculing someone and a sense of humour that can make even your enemy your friend. The best example of the true sense of humour is cartoonist RK Laxman who has excelled in making cartoons of almost all great personalities of our generation. The aim of these works is to make these people laugh at themselves.

If the intentions of the person is to make the dull environment lighter and not hurt the sentiments, it has to be pleasant. If you have a real sense of humour you may save your face at the most difficult period of life.

It may not be so easy to learn the art of having a perfect sense of humour, as the line between humour and mockery is very thin and the only difference is the motive and intention. But once you know it you have enhanced your personality. Learn the art of laughing at your own self. If you have learned the art of admitting your blunders and laughing at your own foolishness you have automatically stopped others from laughing at you. Mahatma Gandhi, when he said about himself that he was the naked fakir, stopped the British government from commenting on his physical traits and dress.

Some people may suggest that you need to be serious with whatever you do, but these suggestions are wrongly taken as if the person should be straight-faced, devoid of a smile and must talk only business. There are many successful businessmen throughout the world who have a perfect sense of humour. The Virgin Airlines chief is remembered for his sense of humour and he does business better than many of the other Airlines.

Let us see in what way we can enhance our personality traits by the right sense of humour:

1. Sense of humour brings down the communication barrier and allows others to consider you as approachable.
2. It can reduce ill-feeling and can create a friendly environment.
3. It can inculcate a sense of confidence to penetrate the ego fence of the other.
4. The right sense of humour can help you to convey some messages without hurting others' feelings.

5. Humour is a terrific guard against hostility and difficult situations.
6. It gives a positive attitude towards others.

If there are so many advantages of being humorous then why can we not try it? There are certain easy ways to make it a part of our life, but it is not always possible to use it at the right time and moment. Prepare yourself for such an effort.

- When you get ready for a party wearing a smart dress, prepare a mental frame of mind to share a moment of laughter with others.
- Whenever you are using humour to bring down the communication barrier make it a point not to use harsh words that can hurt others.
- Prepare yourself with few one-liners that can bring in laughter. It is a way of better communication.
- Do not laugh at your own jokes, allow others to enjoy them too.
- Use old jokes, quotes, cartoons, analogies, observations etc. to bring in the much-needed humour.
- One should never give notice to your audience that you are going to share a joke with them.
- Never pause to give the punch line; you may not get the laugh from your audience every time.
- Make it a point not to use it when someone is making a serious proposal or viewpoint and he is expecting others to listen carefully.

Case Study I

Romesh 'Lucky' was the owner of a very popular eating-place, "EAT and FUN", in Pune. Lucky was a local resident who was very fortunate to reach upto this level. He started as a small teashop owner in the highway. But in a span of twenty years he made a big fortune and his eating joint was one of the most popular ones in the city. He was very popular since his college days and was always a welcome personality in each and every group in the college. He had the capability to make people laugh. When he first opened the teashop, everybody in town was laughing at him for choosing such a career. His tea stall became a favourite place for all commuters to stop and have some snacks and tea. The tea was less important for everyone who stopped, but the hearty laughter they shared was all that drew them. Lucky used to be the centre of attraction for even the older people who visited the shop.

The tea stall became a place of reducing the tension of driving on the highway. Lucky never left the great asset he had. He was gifted with a great sense of humour. His competitors were very upset and used all the sales promotion through various means, but could not succeed. No one could apparently make out the secret of Lucky's success. But the personality of Lucky was the single most important USP for his business. He never allowed success to dictate his behaviour and manned the front desk himself. The excellent behavioural skills of Lucky also motivated other staff members in the restaurant to behave nicely. As the name of the hotel reflected, it was a place of fun for all. There was a nice business environment. It has been heard that the Government of Maharashtra is planning to lease out all the State-owned tourism development hotels to Lucky.

Questions:

1. What was the secret of Lucky?
2. Why cannot the other shopkeepers follow the success route of 'Eat and Fun'?
3. Should Lucky expand his business to other cities?

9

Interpersonal Relationships

It is a proven fact that the effectiveness of a person is highly dependent on his capability to deal with people. Many people with high intellect and competence fail to succeed in the race of life. In real life your success also depends on other external factors. The factor vital for any person to succeed is the relationship with people. There are a few things in our life that we all like to change, but we cannot do much as the result is dependent on others. The relationship between you and other members in the group you belong to or with some other group is called **interpersonal relationship**. There are several members in the group—some may be your peers and friends, others your superiors in the company or in the institution you are, and subordinates who report to you. Therefore, the art is to have an excellent relationship within the group, not only with your superiors, but also with your colleagues and subordinates. Interpersonal skills are not restricted to a small group. They are equally applicable for effective relationships between different groups. The basic relationship can be depicted in a very simple picture like the one shown below:

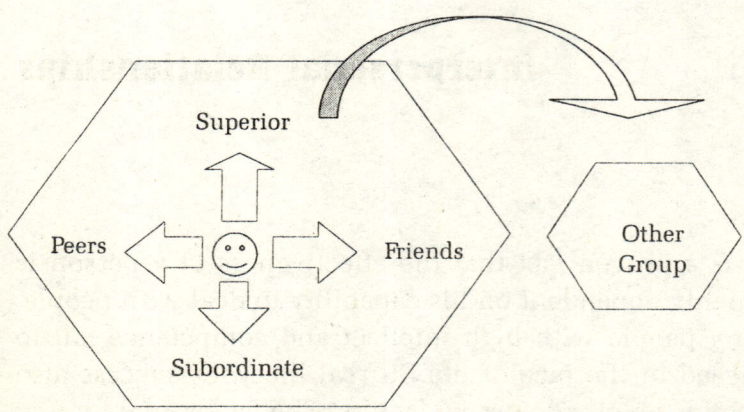

Interpersonal Relationship Hierarchy

Determinants of Interpersonal Relationships

There are several determinants that are important to decide what our behaviour towards other people is. There are several behavioural scientists who have devised models to understand why a person behaves in a unique way with someone. We need to see what the determinants of interpersonal relationships are. They may be listed as under:

1. **Self-analysis:** Human beings are different from all other living beings because they can think and analyse their behaviour. Self-analysis is the strongest of all the determinants that can help a person to improve any relationship to a great extent.
2. **Misperception:** Most of the strain in a relationship is due to a mental box, a frame of mind we are in. The mental frame does not allow us to make our unbiased perception about the other person. The misperception can spoil the relationship.
   Example: When a teacher calls a parent to the school, in anticipation that it must be for addressing a complaint of their son the parents start with a defensive mode. The relationship between the teacher and the parents is determined by such a mental frame.
3. **Selective interactions:** The relationship between individuals in a group can have an adverse effect if the interaction is limited to a sub-group. People always tend to form a sub-set in the larger set of people. Such selective interaction does affect the relationship in the group.
   Example: If a person is attending an official party in a metropolitan city, he may like to find someone from his state talking in the same language and liking the same food, but that can destroy the chance of a good relationship with other persons in the group.
4. **Selective evaluation of other people:** We may evaluate some persons on a biased scale, thereby not developing good relationships. Similarly, at times

people whom we want to boost are evaluated on a higher scale.

Example: The relationship is badly damaged if some rumours or someone else's briefing affects the evaluation of the other person. When a new student joins a class, he meets others in the class with the background of what his roommate has told him about everyone else. He sees the relationship through the eyes of his roommate.

5. **Selective evaluation of self:** We must assess correctly where we stand. If we portray ourselves as what we are not, there is little chance that the relationship will be honest and based on a solid foundation.

Example: The chief of a company feels too important and thinks of himself as more than a normal human being because of his position in the office. He will behave with others in office as if he is the master and others are there to follow him. Even when he is not in the office he has similar feelings and expects the same treatment he gets in office.

Interpersonal Communication: Theories and Concepts

There are four basic theories that can explain the behaviour of a person to others when he is dealing with them. These are:

1. Social Penetration Theory
2. Self-Disclosure
3. Uncertainty Reduction Theory
4. Relational Dialectics Theory

Social Penetration Theory (SPT)

SPT is a theory about the development of 'relational closeness.' Social penetration can help as far as a relationship is concerned. The key points in SPT are that relational closeness can progress from superficial to intimate and that closeness develops through self-disclosure. Closeness varies with factors such as rewards/benefits, costs, vulnerability, satisfaction, stability and security.

Self-Disclosure

'Please listen carefully and try to hear what I am not saying...

What I'd like to be able to say...
What for survival I need to say...
But what I can't say.' —Unknown

In this theory, importance is given to the fact that if you disclose yourself, there shall be a better relationship. Self-disclosure is sharing with someone information that helps him or her in understanding you. Self-disclosure is most revealing when the sharing is in the present and least revealing when the sharing is about the past.—D Johnson, Self-Disclosure Characteristics.

Self-disclosure definitions:
S. Jourard defines self-disclosure as making ourselves 'transparent' to others through our communication, i.e. when we tell others things about ourselves which help them to see our uniqueness as a human being.

Pearce & Sharp make an interesting distinction among three related terms: self-disclosure, confession, and revelation.

Self-disclosure—voluntary communication of information about one's self to another.

Confession—forced or coerced communication of information about one's self to another.

Revelation—unintentional or inadvertent communication of information about one's self to another.

Uncertainty Reduction Theory (URT)

In this theory of relationship, it is presumed that 'the beginning of personal relationships is fraught with uncertainties' and that people want to reduce uncertainty in relationships through knowledge and understanding. To know others we can do it actively, passively or interactively.

Relational Dialectics Theory (RDT)

As per **Baxter**, no relationship can exist by definition unless the parties sacrifice some individual autonomy. However, too much connection paradoxically destroys the relationship because individuals' identities become lost. In RDT, Baxter and **Montgomery** claim that people want a certain amount of mystery and spontaneity in relationships to 'spice things up.' Without variety, the relationship will become dull and too predictable and, therefore, 'emotionally dead.' The key points in this theory are that relationships reflect tensions (conflicts, contradictions) that are played out in communication interaction (dialectical tensions).

Johari Window

This is a conceptual way of studying interpersonal awareness. The name Johari is a combination of the names of two behavioural scientists (Jo+Hari) namely Joseph Luft and Harry Ingham who developed this model. This is a conceptual model to tell how people expose themselves to other people and how receptive they are to the suggestions and feedback from others. There is a window that is divided into four compartments and have four different perspectives, namely:

a) **Arena**: The compartment, in which a person knows the self as well as others. This has openness of mind as far as relationship is concerned.

b) **Blind spot**: It is the area that others know, but the person concerned is not aware of. It may create awkward situations.

c) **Closed area**: It is the compartment in the model where a person is sure of himself, but he does not allow others to know it. He does not allow others to share the information and feelings.

d) **Dark area**: It is the compartment that is neither known to the other person nor to the person in question. This compartment has tremendous scope for improvement.

	Known to self	Unknown to the self
Less ↓ Self-Disclosure ↓ **More**	**Arena** (shared and mutually held, public information, feeling, motives etc.)	**Blind-spot** (Unsuspected information, feeling, reactions etc. known only to the party.)
	Closed (Hidden information, motives, feelings, etc. known only to the self.)	**Dark** (Undiscovered potential and creative reservoir known neither to the self nor to others.)

Feedback: Less → More

- From these we can see that a relationship is mutually useful and trustful if there is a big Arena (I know you, you know me). In this compartment the accurate perceptual judgement will help to develop more realistic mutual expectations. This mutual and satisfying relationship is the basis of a long lasting relationship.
- The expansion of Arena will automatically reduce the compartments of Closed Area (I know, but you do not know). In this Closed Area, the person generally hides the information from others and denies things one knows or feels.
- Blind Spots (I do not know, but you know) will push a person in a relationship where he would like to protect himself from all the ignorance and self-protection mechanism will come into play.

- Arena or Open Area can be increased if we are open to suggestions and feedback from other people.
- Self-disclosure will reveal oneself to others. It is sharing one's own feelings, emotions, facts, knowledge, etc. with others. It is an act that helps a relationship to grow. The act will help to show respect and intimacy to others.
- With proper feedback we know ourselves better. It gives us an opportunity to see ourselves from the other person's viewpoint.

There are several ways in which the Johari Window Analysis of a relationship can help us improve interpersonal relationships. When we know that the relationship is not well, but we cannot do much to know what is wrong, we may do something as under:

1. **Solicit feedback:** One should feel no shame in asking for feedback from the other side.
2. **Initiate self-disclosure:** You can take initiative in telling how you feel about things in question.
3. **Do not defend:** Be ready to listen to negative feedback too. There is no point in defending when you want feedback from others.
4. **Define the mutual expectations:** We must analyse the basis of a relationship and the expectation from such a relationship.
5. **Communicate your concern:** Based on the feedback it is advisable to convey your concern for a better relationship.

TA (TRANSACTIONAL ANALYSIS)

Oxford Dictionary defines transaction as 'a piece of business that is done between people'. In a behavioural science, it is the exchange of communication, both verbal and non-verbal, between two or more individuals. Transaction analysis is the scientific way of studying the state of mind of the persons when he sends or receives the communication.

Transactional Analysis (TA) is psychoanalysis of personality that was developed by psychologists with strong humanist leanings, amongst whom the best known is probably **Eric Berne**, author of *Games People Play* and *What Do You Say After You Say Hello*? Transactional Analysis generally seems to be glossed over in psychology textbooks, both as a form of therapy and as a personality theory. However, people I know, who have tried TA as therapy, have often found that it seems to work. My students also often find that TA offers plausible explanations of interpersonal communication, especially of communication breakdowns, and find it particularly useful in analysing interactions involved in the development of their practical work. Around the late 1950s, Eric Berne began to develop his theories of Transactional Analysis. He said that verbal communication, particularly face-to-face, is at the centre of human social relationships and psychoanalysis. His starting-point was that when two people encounter each other, one of them speaks to the other. This he called the transaction stimulus. The reaction from the other person he called the transaction response.

The person sending the stimulus is called the agent. The person who responds is called the respondent. Transactional Analysis becomes the method of examining the transaction wherein 'I do something to you, and you do something back'.

Berne also says that each person is made up of three alter ego states: Parent, Adult and Child.

In a 'transaction' (an interaction with one or more people), one or the other of these ego states will predominate us as well as other people in the transaction. Particular communicative behaviours are associated with each of these ego states, but it is important to understand that they are not necessarily associated with chronological stages of psychological development. An adult can exhibit child-like communicative behaviour and a child can exhibit adult-like behaviour. The complete personality diagram of any human being encompasses everything he may feel, think, say or do.

Components of Ego States

If we examine peoples' personality more closely, we do not discover more ego states, but we may discover components of those ego states. Berne accepts that the Parental ego state proves to be composed of two states, one deriving from the mother and the other from the father. Further, within the Child ego state we will find Parent, Adult and Child states.

It is important to realise that, although we will be looking at each of these ego states in turn, there is no implication that we would use only one in a transaction. It is quite likely that we will move from one to the other, since we all have these three ego states as part of our personality.

Transactional Analysis is one of the most commonly studied theories of modern psychology. The transaction between two groups is always a necessity. Whether a person is in business, a teacher, a parent, a social worker or runs a fast food stall, Eric Berne's very interesting theory will enrich ones dealings with people and understanding of oneself. Throughout history and from all standpoints—philosophy, medical science, religion—people have believed that each man and woman has a multiple nature.

Transactional Analysis: The Theoretical Background

In the early twentieth century, Sigmund Freud first established that the human psyche is multi-faceted and that each of us has warring factions in our subconscious. Many theories have come up in the last century, new theories are continuously being put forward, all concentrating on the essential conviction that each one of us has parts of our personality which surface and affect our behaviour according to different circumstances.

In 1951, **Dr Wilder Penfield** began a series of scientific experiments. He concluded that the human brain acts like a tape recorder and whilst we may 'forget' experiences, the brain still has them recorded. Along with events the brain also records the associated feelings, and both feelings and events stay locked together.

It is possible for a person to exist in two states simultaneously (because persons replaying hidden events and feelings could talk about them objectively at the same time). Hidden experiences when replayed are vivid, and affect how we feel at the time of replaying. There is a certain connection between mind and body, i.e., the link between the biological and the psychological, e.g., a psychological fear of spiders and a biological feeling of nausea.

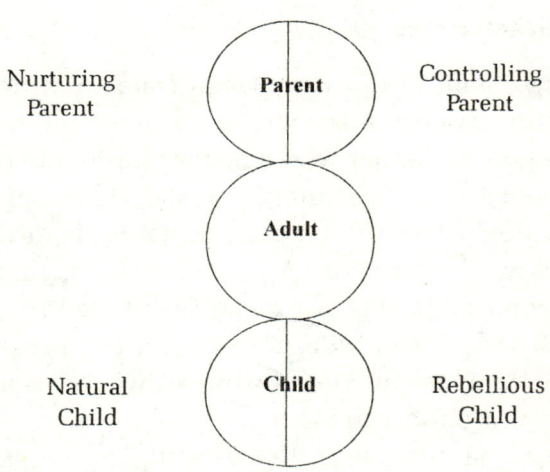

Nurturing Parent   Controlling Parent

Natural Child   Rebellious Child

Parent

This is our voice of authority, absorbed conditioning, learning and attitudes from when we are young. We are conditioned by our parents, teachers, elders, next door neighbours, aunts and uncles. Our Parent ego state is made up of a huge number of hidden and overt recorded playbacks typically embodied by phrases and attitudes starting with 'how to', 'under no circumstances', 'always', 'never forget', 'don't lie, cheat, steal', etc. Our parent ego state is formed by external events and influences as we grow through early childhood. We can change it, but doing so is not easy. These are the physical expressions of parent ego state–angry or impatient body language and expressions, finger pointing, patronising gestures. The verbal communication will include—'always', 'never', 'once and for all', judgmental words, critical words, patronising language.

Parent Characteristics

The first ego state is the Parent ego state in which the person who is communicating is passing on the instruction just as a father who tells his children to do and not to do something. The Parent ego state is the mode of communication when the sender is communicating with a command and instruction. A person when saying, 'you must keep your table neat and clean' is talking in a parent ego state. If the person who is receiving the instruction responds with 'what can I do, the office sweeper is always late,' he is in a child ego state.

We are all familiar with the parent. The parent is a status figure who has the power to direct other persons' lives by means of demanding conformity to certain behavioural norms, reinforced with sanctions or rewards. As we grow up, we learn our parents' behaviour patterns and communication styles, and then apply them ourselves. This does not, of course, imply that we have to be parents to use these communication styles. A child may adopt the Parent ego state in a transaction with its toys or other people, a man may adopt it in a transaction with his girlfriend and, naturally, a parent may adopt it in a transaction with his or her own child.

The Nurturing Parent and Controlling Parent

Berne distinguishes between the Nurturing (or Natural) Parent and the Controlling Parent. Essentially, the Nurturing Parent's characteristics are quite positive, but can be overbearing and limiting. The Nurturing Parent is concerned with his child's welfare. So he rewards, protects and cares for the child and tries to pass on good moral standards—'always be on time', 'save your money', 'work hard' are some of the typical examples given by Berne. The Nurturing Parent can help the child feel okay about his relationships, but can also be overprotective, smothering the child's development.

The Controlling Parent is a different type of parent, who wants to command, instruct and pass judgements. This Parent is strict and judgmental, is quick to form opinions about the child's behaviour, may even have formed the judgements before the behaviour, and sees to it that the child should succeed on the parent's terms.

Communication Behaviour

The Nurturing Parent is likely to use comforting phrases, such as 'don't worry, it will be okay' or 'let me see if I can help you with that', as well as offering frequent praise. The Controlling Parent will offer quite a number of orders, which, if necessary will be justified by appeal to some kind of moral criteria or principles of behaviour which appear to have some kind of absolute value. This verbal behaviour will of course be paralleled by appropriate non-verbal behaviour: encouraging gestures, indulgent smiles in the case of the Nurturing Parent, hostile glares and fixed stares in the case of the Controlling Parent.

Example: Bosses are generally a typical example of Parent ego state. At times he may assure that a hard working executive is 'a highly valued member of the team'. But when the same boss is confronted with the open hostility of the worker's union, he may tell them they would not receive a pay-rise again. He may invite an unhappy worker as union representative, who has refused to accept the unlawful working hours he is trying to force on them. He disdainfully accuses the worker for spoiling the working environment of the office. He can use abusive words to bully some unfortunate individual. Bosses generally are in a Parent state, whether nurturing or controlling.

Child

Our internal reactions and feelings to external events form the 'Child'. This is the seeing, hearing, feeling, and emotional body of data within each of us. When anger or despair dominate reason, the Child is in control. Like our Parent we can change it, but it is not easy. These are the physical expressions of Child ego state—sad expressions, despair, temper tantrums, whining voice, rolling eyes, shrugging shoulders, teasing, delight, laughter, speaking behind hand, raising hand to speak, squirming and giggling. The verbal expressions are baby talk—'I wish'

'I want', 'I don't care', 'oh no', 'not again, things never go right for me', 'worst day of my life', 'bigger', 'biggest', 'best', and many superlatives to impress.

Adult

'Adult' is the most sensible ego state. It is the ability to think and determine action for ourselves based on received data. The Adult in us begins to form at around ten months old, and is the means by which we keep our Parent and Child under control. These are the physical expressions of adult ego state—attentive, interested, straightforward, tilted head, non-threatening and non-threatened. The verbal expressions of adult ego state are—'why', 'what', 'how', 'who', 'where', 'when', 'how much', 'in what way', comparative expressions, reasoned statements, true, false, 'probably', 'possibly', 'I think', 'I realise', 'I see', 'I believe', 'in my opinion'.

Effectiveness of Transaction

There are several modes of transaction, but the best is one that is complementary. If the two transacting persons are complementing the ego state, the communication will progress in the right direction otherwise it will end in a stalemate. There is no general rule as to the effectiveness of any ego state in any given situation. Some people get results by being dictatorial (Parent to Child), or by throwing temper tantrums (Child to Parent), but for a balanced approach to life, Adult to Adult is generally recommended.

Transactional Analysis is effectively a language within a language—a language of true meaning, feeling and motive. It can help you in every situation, firstly through being able to understand more clearly what is going on, and secondly, by virtue of this knowledge, we give ourselves choices of what ego states to adopt, which signals to send, and where to send them. This enables us to make the most of all our communications and therefore create, develop and maintain better relationships.

The most sensible and nice way of communication is when there is communication between two persons in the adult ego state. The communication between two groups of persons in a business meeting is a communication between two adult ego states.

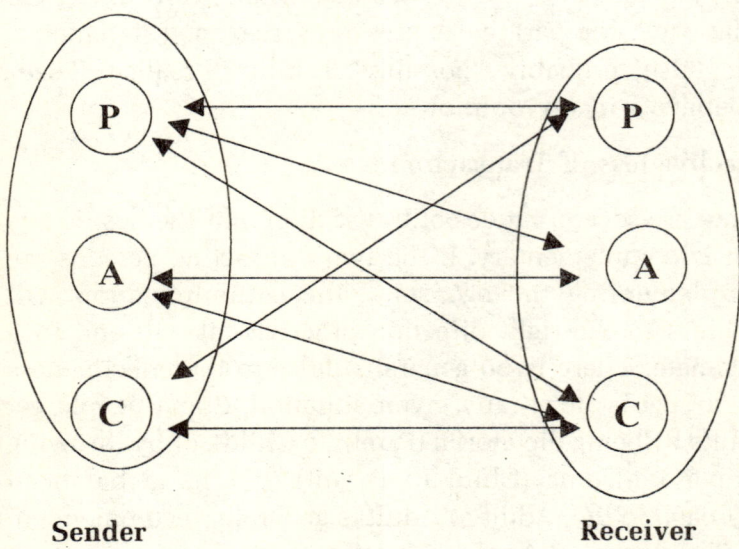

The above figure shows a transaction between two groups of persons. It depicts different modes of transactions (exchange) between the sender and receiver.

a) If the transaction is between P and P, that is between two persons only trying to command and dominate, then there shall in all possibility be a communication full of harsh talk and chances of confrontation are very high. Examples of such communication are the debates in a court-room where both lawyers are arguing to score points over the other. In our day-to-day life such a transaction is not a welcome state.

b) The transaction between P and A is very common in office environment where there is one boss and few subordinates. The boss will pass on the instructions to the subordinates, who in turn will follow that.

c) The transaction between A and A is a very sensible way of communicating. Both the groups are receptive to each other and talk logically. Such transaction can result in an effective and fruitful communication. Example of such communication can be between two diplomats negotiating an international issue of common concern.

d) The other transaction, which is very ineffective and one we need to avoid, is the transaction between C and C ego states. In such a transaction, the response as well as the original communication is irresponsible. The person who is sending such communication is also not very sensibly using the transaction. Example of such transaction is communication between two drunk persons in a bar. They start a conversation with, 'this world is very funny and all the persons in the city are jokers'. At this the response from the other person is 'God is not kind to human being and has created this city to make fun of his own creation.'

The other kind of transaction is between P to C, a person is instructing but the person receiving it does not take it in the right spirit. A boss comes and says, 'We must adhere to the deadlines.' Hearing this the subordinate says, 'Sir, you always pressurise us with impractical deadlines.'

If we are to change our Parent or Child we must do so through our Adult. In other words: P is our 'Taught' concept of life, A is our 'Thought' concept of life, C is our 'Felt' concept of life.

When we communicate, we are doing so from one of our own alter ego states, Parent, Adult or Child. Our feelings at the time determine which one we use, and at any time something can trigger a shift from one state to another. When we respond, we are also doing this from one of the three states, and it is in the analysis of these stimuli and responses that the essence of Transactional Analysis lies.

At the core of Berne's theory is the rule that effective transactions (i.e. successful communication) must be complementary. They must go back from the receiving ego state to the sending ego state. For example, if the stimulus is Parent to Child, the response must be Child to Parent, If the transaction is 'crossed', there will be a problem between sender and receiver. If a crossed transaction occurs, there is ineffective communication. Worse still, either or both parties will be upset. For the relationship to continue smoothly the agent or the respondent must rescue the situation with a complementary transaction. In serious breakdowns, there is no chance of immediately resuming a discussion about the original subject matter. Attention is focused on the relationship. The discussion can only continue constructively when and if the relationship is mended.

When we are trying to identify ego states, words are only part of the story. To analyse a transaction you need to see and feel what is being said as well.

- 7 per cent of meaning is in the words spoken.
- 38 per cent of meaning is paralinguistic (the way that the words are said).
- 55 per cent is in the facial expression.

SHARPEN YOUR INTERPERSONAL SKILLS

It may be very easy to mould your action because it is very much in your control, but a person who can have positive influence on others is the one having interpersonal relationship skills. There are few basic methods of influencing others.

We all are a sub-set of the larger set in society, which has several individuals with different tastes, likes and their own identity. We all want to have a positive influence on other people in our personal and professional lives. We do this with the motive of forming new business ties, keeping customers, maintaining friendships, changing behaviour, or improving marriage and family relationships. But it is certainly essential for all of us to maintain and nourish this important relationship.

There are some easy ways we can do it. We may like to influence the lives of other people and do it powerfully and ethically. If we categorise, we may arrive at three basic categories of influence:

- Model by example (others see): We are highly influenced by the public faces in society. The cinema artist and sports personality has always been a role model for the younger generation. This is how a leader should influence the others.
- Build caring relationships (others feel): This is an emotional bonding and the person is highly influenced by what he feels. This is very useful for persons who are sensitive to their emotional needs.
- Mentor by instruction (others hear): Many a times we may not see a person, but still the person can have a positive influence on us by hearing from some other source.

The following methods of influence fall under the above mentioned three categories.

Never talk negative and unkind words

We do talk negative and harsh when we are frustrated, tired and fed up with our own problems. We must refrain from saying unkind or negative words, particularly when we are provoked or fatigued. In these circumstances, not to say unkind or critical things is a supreme form of self-mastery. Courage is quality at its highest testing point. If we have no model of restraint to follow, we will take out our frustration on our fellow workers. We may need to find new models, new examples to follow, and learn to win our own battles privately, to get our motives straight, to gain perspective and control, and to back away from impulsively speaking or striking out.

Do not allow personal ego to dictate relationships

We may not be happy with the performance of an individual but that should not affect the relationship. We must distinguish between the person and the behaviour or performance. While we may disapprove of bad behaviour and poor performance, we first need to communicate and help build a sense of intrinsic worth and self-esteem totally apart from comparisons and judgements. Doing this will powerfully inspire superior effort. The power to distinguish between person and performance and to communicate intrinsic worth flows naturally out of our own sense of intrinsic worth.

Exercise patience with others

In times of stress, our impatience surfaces. We may say things we do not really mean or intend to say. Or we may become sullen, communicating through emotion and attitude, rather than words, eloquent messages of criticism, judgement and rejection. We then harvest hurt feelings and strained relationships. Patience is the practical expression of faith, hope, wisdom and love. It is a very active emotion. It is not indifference, sullen endurance or resignation. Patience is emotional diligence. We nurture any relationship with great care and if we do not have patience we may lose the same.

Never advertise the good you do to others

We should perform anonymous service. If we are doing good for others anonymously, our sense of intrinsic worth and self-respect increases. We must do it without expectation of publicity or reward. Selfless service has always been one of the most powerful methods of influence.

Promises made to others are to be kept

We must know that when we say something it is like a contract we have with the person. It is generally a termination in relationship if we have not kept it. If you cannot keep it do not commit it. By making and keeping our promises, we win friends. It is good to make promises (resolutions, commitments, oaths and covenants), but never make a promise you will not keep.

Focus on the circle of influence

There are some things which are well within our control and there are a few not in our control. We need to increase our area of influence by focusing on the requirement of others. As we focus on doing something positive about the things we can control, we expand our circle of influence.

Changing our habits of doing and thinking solves direct control problems. Indirect control problems require us to change our methods of influence. For instance, we complain from time to time, 'if only the boss could understand my problem.' But few of us take the time to prepare the kind of presentation that the boss would listen to and respect, in his language, with his problems in mind. With no control problems, we can control our reaction to them, deciding within ourselves how anything or anybody will affect us. As William James said: 'We can change our circumstances by a mere change of our attitude.'

THE IMPORTANCE OF CARING IN A RELATIONSHIP

Faith is the foundation of a relationship. We must treat all people around as faithful and never doubt their intentions. There are chances that ninety-five percent of the people around us are faithful and only a very few of them are unfaithful. Just think, should the five percent of unfaithful persons guide your behaviour towards the ninety-five percent faithful? We must assume that good faith produces good fruit. If we think that others want and mean to do their best, as they say it, we can expect and bring out the best in them. Our efforts to classify, categorise, judge and measure, often emerge from our own insecurities and frustrations in dealing with complex, changing realities. Each person has many dimensions and different potential, some evident, most dormant. And they tend to respond to how we treat them and what we believe about them. Some may let us down or take advantage of our trust, considering us naïve or gullible, but most will come through, simply because we believe in them. Whenever we assume good faith, born of good motives and inner security, we appeal to the good in others.

Goethe said: 'Treat a man as he is, and he will remain as he is. Treat a man as he can and should be, and he will become as he can and should be.'

Example: There were only a few cricketers in the world who were engaged in match fixing, but when the allegations started coming it was free for all. The doubts in the mind were enough to spoil the gentleman image of the popular game of cricket.

Try to understand others first. We have our own preconceived notions about most things. We behave according to these notions. Seek first to understand, then to be understood. When we are communicating with another, we need to give full attention, to be completely present. Then we need to empathise and 'walk in his moccasins' for a while. This takes courage and patience. But until people feel that you understand them, they will not be open to your influence.

Example: Anil went to a Public bank to get a demand draft for his son in some other city. He got it after three hours, and was furious with the service. He used foul language at the front desk official for not putting a 'only A/C payee' stamp on it. The person was facing a similar hostile long queue since morning as it was pay day for a local factory. The other help desk personnel was on sudden casual leave and it was a tough day for the bank personnel. The unwanted fight could have easily been avoided had Anil understood the agony of the bank employee.

Encourage openness, honest expressions. We expect others to be transparent, honest and faithful. These qualities can help a relationship be strong and everlasting. Too often we punish honest, open expressions or questions. We upbraid, judge, belittle, and embarrass people. Others learn to cover up, to protect themselves, and not to ask. The greatest single barrier to rich, honest communication is the tendency to criticise and judge. We are required to give an understanding response. By using the understanding response (reflecting feeling), three good things happen:

1. You gain increased understanding and clarity of feelings and problems,
2. You gain new courage and growth and
3. You build real confidence in the relationship.

This response has its greatest value when a person wants to talk about a situation laden with emotions and feelings. But note that this response is more of an attitude than a technique. It will fail if you are trying to manipulate another. It will work if you deeply want to understand.

Example: The principal of Jadavpur university called all the second year mechanical students for bunking second half classes to see a football match between the favourite teams in Kolkata. The class representative Sunil was honest enough to tell the principal the truth, and they apologised for their behaviour but the principal fined all the students. Was the open expression well rewarded?

Try to repair a relationship, apologise. Try and show genuine effort to repair a strained relationship. If you are offended, take the initiative. If someone offends you unknowingly and continues to do so, take the initiative to clear it up. Consider two tragic consequences of not taking the initiative: first, the offended one often broods about the offence until the situation is blown out of proportion; and second, we then behave defensively to avoid being hurt further. When taking the initiative, do it in good spirit, not in a spirit of vindication and anger. Also, describe your feelings when and how you were offended rather than judging or labelling the other person. This preserves the dignity and self-respect of the other, who then can respond and learn without feeling threatened. All that is needed from your side is to admit your mistakes, apologise and ask for forgiveness.

Example: Many marital relationships get strained to the extent of divorce because both partners do not want to repair the hurt feeling. If you said something in a fit of anger, come forward and sincerely apologise. Soothing the hurt feeling can reduce tension between enemy countries; it can certainly help the fighting couple build an amicable relationship.

There is no use of arguments. Generally we want to defend our ego by arguing for the sake of argument. Dale Carnegie has very correctly said that in an argument you are a loser if you win the argument, as you have lost a good friend, and if you lose the argument you are a loser anyway. We must never argue for anything, a polite way of expressing your feelings is more than sufficient than trying to win an argument. Covey has said, 'Let arguments fly out open windows'. Give no answer to contentious arguments or irresponsible accusations. Let such things 'fly out open windows' until they spend themselves. If you try to answer or reason, you only serve to gratify and ignite pent-up hostility and anger. When you go quietly about your business, the other person has to struggle with the natural consequences of irresponsible expression. Do not be drawn into any poisonous, contentious orbit, or you will find yourself bitten and afflicted similarly.

Do not expect the other person to change. By no means can we change any person as we want him or her to be. God has made all of us with some unique qualities. If we want a person to change as we think it will be good for our relationship, we are doing a business exchange rather than relationship building. Such a conditional relationship will never last long. Covey said, 'Accept the person and the situation.' The first step in changing or improving another is to accept him as he is. Nothing reinforces defensive behaviour more than judgement, comparison or rejection. A feeling of acceptance and worth frees a person from the need to defend and helps release the natural growth tendency to improve. Acceptance is not condoning a weakness or agreeing with an opinion. Rather, it is affirming the intrinsic worth of another by acknowledging that he does feel or think a particular way.

THE RULES FOR PASSING INSTRUCTIONS

1. **Before you start speaking, words and actions must be well prepared.** What we say may be less important

than how we say it. Before we speak anything harsh we must rethink. When a child returns from school full of its own needs, stop and get control on what you need to say to him. Choose pleasantness and cheerfulness. We need to give full attention to his needs. Doing something good for others, even in your family, can change the environment of the whole house. Choosing to be your best self will arrest fatigue and renew your best resolves.

Example: Rudra came back from school with his results for class ten. His father has always expected him to score more than 80 per cent in his exams. The results were not to the expectations of his father. Rudra was upset and hesitant to tell his father that he could score only 68 per cent as his marks in literature were not good. But he scored 98 per cent in his science subjects. At the dinner table Rudra's father was critical of his performance. He called him worthless and never thought to say a few encouraging words for his good performance in the science subjects.

2. **We must try to resolve the differences.** If we are powerful, generally we try to sort out the differences by saying harsh words and trying to dominate the other person. Bulldozing others with rude words is the most common way to settle a difference. But if you are weak you will try to avoid the unpleasant situation. Covey said, 'Many people either fight or flight when they disagree. Fighting takes many forms, ranging from violence and open expressions of anger and hate to subtle sarcasm, sharp answers, clever

comebacks, belittling humour, judgements and reactions.'

Example: In a worker's union meeting the issue of a proposed strike by the union to put forward the demands of the workers was being discussed. Mohan, a new employee did not want to participate in the strike, as he feared the loss of his job as a disciplinary action for striking workers. He was avoiding the situation and did not attend the meeting. On the strike day he tried to attend the factory. The union leaders did not take it lightly and threatened him with dire consequences. Mohan did not say anything, but he had an urge for revenge to his insult. All this could have been avoided had he gone to the leaders with a proposal and his problems of participating in the strike.

3. **Do not protect people for their actions.** Every person likes to see what he has done. It gives him or her a sense of some achievement even if it is not to his choice. If you want a dignified relationship, it is unkind to shield people from the consequences of their own behaviour. In doing so, we teach them that they are inadequate and weak. This is generally to show that we love and care for them, but in fact it will give them a sense of unfulfilled desire to face the result of their action. A mother is very caring for her child and would like to protect her baby from all the bad things in this world. But have you ever thought that not allowing her to face the pain of falling on the ground may defer her learning process. In the process she is also doing more harm than good.

Example: At a family gathering an uncle who has just returned from London, asked his nephew Rohit about his performance in the school final exam. As soon as the question was put up and even before Rohit could frame an answer, Rohit's mother replied that he got star marks in all the papers and he could still have done better had he gone for his coaching to a better institute. The fact was that Rohit could get marks just sufficient for first class. Rohit was not ashamed of his performance but his mother's blatant lie belittled his achievement and he was feeling ashamed of what he could have achieved.

4. **Be there at the crossroads.** None of us want the people we care most about, to make decisions that have important long-range consequences on the basis of short-range emotional perspectives and moods, personal insecurity and self-doubt. How can we influence them? First, think before you act. Do not be controlled by your own short-range emotional moods and by doing something that injures whatever relationship and influence you have. Second, understand that people tend to act in terms of how they feel instead of what they know. Motivation is more a function of the heart than the head. When we sense that our language of reason and logic is not communicating with their language of sentiment and emotion, we should try to understand their language as we would a foreign tongue, without condemning or rejecting them. This effort communicates respect and acceptance, lowers defences, diminishes the

need to fight, and restores the desire to do what is right.

5. **Speak the languages of logic and emotion.** The language of logic and the language of emotion are as different as English and French. When we realise that we do not have a common language, we need to communicate in one of the four other ways:
   - Give time, for when we cheerfully give time, we transfer its worth to another;
   - Be patient, as patience also communicates worth and says, 'I'll go at your speed; I'm happy to wait for you; you're worth it';
   - Seek to understand, because an honest effort to understand eliminates the need to fight and to defend; and
   - Openly express your feelings and be congruent with your non-verbal expressions.

6. **Delegate effectively.** Effective delegation takes emotional courage as we allow, to one degree or another, others to make mistakes on our time, money and good name. This courage consists of patience, self-control, faith in the potential of others, and respect for individual differences. Effective delegation must be two-way: responsibility is given, responsibility is received. There are three phases. First is the initial agreement. People have a clear understanding of what is expected and what the resources, authority, latitude and guidelines are. Second, sustaining the delegates. The supervisor becomes a source of help, the

advocate, and not the feared adversary. He provides resources, removes obstacles, sustains actions and decisions, gives vision, provides training, and shares feedback. Third is the accountability process. It is largely one of self-evaluation, since delegates are supervised by results and actual performance.

7. **Involve people in meaningful projects.** Meaningful projects have a healing influence on people. However, what is meaningful to a manager may be meaningless to a subordinate. Projects take on meaning when people are involved in the planning and thinking processes. We all need to be engaged in a good cause. Without such projects, life loses its meaning; in fact, the life span is short for people who retire, looking for a tensionless state. Life is sustained by tension between where we are now and where we want to be.

8. **We reap what we sow.** If we make people understand that as nature will give them what they sow, in our own life we will get the rewards of what action we have taken to give shape to our future. We must train all the people the law of harvest. We teach the 'agricultural principles' of preparing the soil, seeding, cultivating, watering, weeding, and harvesting. We focus on natural processes. We align the systems, especially compensation, to reflect and reinforce this idea.

9. **Let natural consequences teach responsible behaviour.** One of the kindest things we can do is to let the natural or logical consequences of people's actions teach them responsible behaviour. They may

not like it or us, but popularity is a fickle standard by which to measure character development. We care enough for their growth and security to suffer their displeasure.

10. **The relationship fails because** overcoming the generally committed mistakes is essential for any relationship to grow. In our attempts to influence others, we commonly make mistakes.

Blunder #1: Understand before Advise. We generally rush to advise and instruct others for what we feel is right. The advice will have an impact only if there is some sort of confidence and proper understanding. In issuing such advice we first need to establish an understanding relationship. Unless we understand the unique situation and feelings of the other person, we will not know how to advise or counsel him. The cure is very simple and it is to show empathy (not sympathy). We need to understand, than to be understood.

Blunder #2: Do not expect others to change. The relationship cannot last long if it is based on conditions and if we expect others to change for us. Attempt to build/rebuild relationships without changing conduct or attitude. As Emerson so aptly put it, 'What you are shouts so loudly in my ears I can't hear what you say.' Cure: Show consistency and sincerity.

Blunder #3: Assume that good example and relationship is sufficient. We assume that a good example and a good relationship are sufficient, that we do not need to explicitly teach people. Just as vision without love contains no motivation, so also love without vision contains no goals, no guidelines, no standards, and no lifting power. Cure: Teach and talk about vision, mission, roles, goals, guidelines and standards.

10

Enhance Your Effectiveness

Have you ever given a thought to evaluate your performance in day-to-day activities and analysed whether your performance is based on the parameters of effectiveness or not? We know from our childhood that whatever we do, we should handle it efficiently. We are expected to do more volume of work in less time. Even if we are very busy doing something or the other we may fall in the category of very efficient but not effective! The focus is limited to the immediate goal. The concepts of being effective are as under:

1. An effective person is more likely to be focused on the result. Even though we may be very busy throughout the day we may not prove to be effective if the result is negative or zero at the end of the day. An executive working for a company travelling around the city,

meeting several clients but with no closing of sales, will be a busy but ineffective salesman.
2. An effective person is more likely to accomplish the result with some ways and means with which purists may not agree. He will not be bound to the rulebooks.
3. An effective person is more likely to have a long-term perspective and he will like to achieve the long-term goal as earmarked in the clear objective he has.

How to reach your goal effectively

Habit 1: Be pro-active

- Most of us are supposedly efficient if we react to any need fast and promptly. In a country where the services are not at all rendered, it is nice to get a service which is prompt and responsive to your need. But we are going a step further and saying that you need to be pro-active. When we say pro-active it means anticipating your need beforehand and start preparing for the outcome. We are required to execute the plans as deemed fit.
- Do not blame circumstances or conditions for your behaviour—we always try to find some external factors to shield our failures. If the tree is not growing the peasant will blame irregular rainwater. An effective person will arrange water from any source but will ensure the proper watering of the tree.
- Accept your responsibility—the responsibility given to you has to be kept above all hindrances.

Enhance Your Effectiveness

An effective person will always welcome any responsibility and will not shirk from it.
- Focus your effort on the circle of Influence: the cirde of Influence is the area where we can contribute. It is a big world and there is opportunity for all of us but what we are presently doing is all that matters. If you are a research student and are devoting all your time in a club activity you are certainly not focusing on your goal.
- Work on which you can do something.

Habit 2: Begin with end in Mind

- Start with a clear understanding of your destination. We all have some dreams and we want to achieve these dreams. Based on what we think, we set some goals for ourselves. The short term goals set by us if combined can lead us to a destination we would like to be in few years time from now.
- We need to understand where we stand today and what the road map is to reach our destination. If we are risk-avoiding persons we will not like to find our own road map and will follow the beaten track of other persons. The challenges we take will enable us to be strong enough to face adverse situations.
- Understand that the process of performance has two stages. The first stage is the stage when you have overcome the mental barrier and that this work can be done. You have visualised the process to perform it. The second stage is when you have

decided to implement the plans and you start doing it physically, which is the second creation.
- The goals you have set for yourself are high and you need a ladder to climb it. The ladder must be the right size and of course it must lean on the right walls.

Habit 3: Fix up your priority

- This has to do with time management and priorities in life. You are required to do several things at the same time of which some are important while others are not so important. There are also many things that simply waste your time and energy. For a daily routine job we need to fix priorities.
- We need to identify work which may need immediate attention, and the work which is related to success and failure in our life.

   Example: You have to appear for your university examination next week. There are six papers in the examinations. You curtail other activities and focus on the exam devoting most of the time in the day only for studies. You have to identify the subjects which need more time, and the subjects that you can manage without much difficulty. Time management will help you avoid the rushing and nervous feeling just before the exams. Have you noticed some of the students are very confident and a picture of self-belief, whereas there are others sweating, feeling nervous and shaky. You decide which one is the better way of preparation.

Habit: 4 Seek first to understand and then to be understood

We are eager to analyse any issue and conclude for ourselves without bothering about what others feel. We must understand the problems being faced by others. We see any situation from our own view point and conclude what we think as right, but we can have a better working solution if we seek to understand the view points of others on issues of conflict.

Listen not with ears alone, but also with your eyes and heart.

The greatest need of a human being is psychological survival. Have you seen any one pleading innocence and the policeman simply not willing to listen simply because he is a bully who does not have any consideration for the feelings of others? We have a deep desire of the following:

- To be understood
- To be appreciated
- To be affirmed
- To be validated

Most of us are habituated to suggest to others what they should do and what is right. We rush to any conclusion without bothering to find out what the other person has to say or feels. Your effectiveness can be greatly improved if you can diagnose before prescribing.

There is a famous Greek philosophy that is embodied in the three stages of dealing with others. We need to assess our own ability, then the feelings of others and finally the reasons for doing this.

1. Ethos–Your Personal ability.
2. Pathos–Feeling
3. Logos–Reasoning

The more deeply you understand other people, the more you will appreciate them.

Habit: 5 Think Win-Win

When you are dealing with persons with a motive of defeating others and proving your superiority by uttering something to hurt them, it is bound to affect the relationship. If you want to share your victory with the other person your actions will not damage the relationship.

- This is fundamental to success in all our interactions.
- Traditional authoritarian supervision is a win/lose proposition.
- Win—Win implies focus on results and not method.
- This involves:
  1. See the problem from the other's point of view.
  2. Identify the key issues and concerns (not position).
  3. What results would constitute fully acceptable solutions?
  4. Identify possible new options to achieve those results.

Make your presence felt

In this world where there is a mad rush of people to achieve greater heights, silent workers are not noticed.

Even though you may be slogging and working hard, your contribution may not be recognised by your superiors. In such times you need to present your work nicely and be visible. It is equally important to do it nicely and in a sober way otherwise people will label you a show-off.

Adopt a practical approach

In a work place the first person whom you need to sell your ideas to is your boss. You are an internal supplier and he is an internal customer. Whenever you get a deadline from your boss, be practical. Try to give your best without compromising on quality. Impressing others with an ambitious project with lots of investment does not always work.

Be polite but assertive

People who get the opportunity to work are fortunate. Therefore never say 'no' to any job that has been assigned to you. Know your limits and if it is getting beyond it, you must talk to your boss in a straight and honest manner. People will appreciate your honesty and would like to help you out.

Do not remain engrossed in routine job

The more time you take to do a routine job, the less you excel in non-routine jobs. Experts say that you must spend 20 per cent of your time doing routine jobs and 80 per cent of your time performing non-routine functions such as thinking, planning, programming, problem-solving, influencing others and decision-making. It is important to delegate the routine jobs to your juniors and allow them to do it freely.

Never say 'no' to any job assigned

Your actions must reflect that you are capable, confident and ready to take more responsibility. Whenever you are discussing your capabilities try to be self-critical. Bring about a feel good factor so that your team mates enjoy your company. See that they talk to you freely and share a personal rapport with them. Every job has two sides to it —Technical side (Hardware skills) and Trans-Technical side (Soft-skills). Technical competence and knowledge are the skills required to accomplish a job. Trans-Technical skill is the art of dealing with people and influencing those who work with you and around you.

Put your goals into writing

There is something undeniably powerful about writing out what you want, getting your dream out of your head and on to a piece of paper. It then seems more practical. It's a stronger declaration of what you are working towards, rather than having a vague, flimsy notion floating around in your head.

Be specific with your goals.

Many do not get what they truly want in their lives because they are too vague about what they want. It is not enough to say 'I want more money' or 'I want to be rich'. Instead, you decide, 'I want Rs 1,00,000'. You now have a clear target to shoot for.

Set a deadline

Did you ever set a New Year's resolution and broken it? Most people have. And most people fail to achieve their dreams because they did not include a deadline with their goal. Deadlines move us to action.

Case Study I

Mrs Renuka Sen is a lady doctor in the local hospital. Her husband Dr Amitabh Sen is also a famous surgeon in the City Apollo hospital. He is extremely busy with his practice and the hospital he is working for. Recently, the Medical Council of India as well as an International medical body has honoured him with an international award. To celebrate the prize he invited all the famous persons of the city to his residence for a party. Dr Sen prepared a guest list of fifty eminent people in the city. He was particularly concerned that the invited guests should be extended the best of hospitality. Mrs Renuka herself was given the responsibility of arranging everything. She had to take the day off from her hospital. She was working carefully to arrange everything from caterer to decorator as per the details she had worked out for the day.

She also had to prepare a few special dishes for dinner in the evening. She was on her toes throughout the day. The guests started arriving on time and the party was organised in the best possible way. The dinner was ready and guests started to take their dinner, but the food being prepared with great care under the supervision of Renuka was not as per the expectation of Dr Sen. He was furious with his wife. As soon as the guests left, Dr Sen showed his anger and they both started an unending argument on what should have been done. Renuka was especially very sad that in spite of her best effort she could not make it a memorable evening. Dr Sen was also not happy as many of the guests did not turn up and there was substantial wastage of food.

Questions:

1. Was the delegation of all the responsibility to Renuka right or not?
2. Where did the organising of the party go wrong?
3. Was the attitude towards Renuka shown by Dr Sen right?
4. What could have saved the unpleasant situation as mentioned above?

11

Time Management—Organise Yourself

We know that an effective person has to utilise his time perfectly to meet schedules and deadlines. Time for everyone in this universe is the same but some people find it sufficient and others say it is always scarce. Some people always complain that they are too busy, deeply engrossed in their work. But their better performing colleagues find sufficient time to complete the work. At the same time they even find time to spend with their family. As a student in an examination you must have noticed a few candidates always find it difficult to finish the papers in the allotted three hours whereas some complete it in two hours and still get better marks. The reason is better time management. To become effective you must know the essence of 'Putting First Things First'.

Managing your time well is not only relevant for an executive but even for a housewife who has to manage her house well. The effective management of time can make your personality impressive as it can remove hesitancy, boost confidence and prevent sudden rushing for any activity. Persons who are poised and balanced are confident they will not need to rush for the final deadlines. If you are a regular reader of your course, you are not required to burn the midnight oil. This habit of 'putting first things first' centres on many questions relating to life and time management.

There are two factors which, if managed properly, can help a person to be organised greatly. The great behavioural scientist Covey has identified two vital factors that can define an activity—'Urgent' and 'Important'.

- 'Urgent'—are the activities that you cannot keep on hold and you have to pay your attention to. These activities require immediate attention, such as the ringing of the phone or leakage of a tap etc. Although we might not have planned for it we are required to leave aside the job we have in hand to take up this.
- 'Important'—are the jobs that are required to be prioritised above other tasks as the completion of these will affect the final result of the entire work. Say an examinee is to clear an exam. The three hours of written exam is the most important activity for him at that particular period. His

preparation shall depend on the performance of those three hours. These activities are to be done with results.

Crisis Deadline Driven Projects I	**Preventive** & Planning Activities II
Interruptions Mail Phone Calls III	**Trivial** Phone calls etc. IV

The above shown matrix is the Time Management Matrix, which shows the classification of jobs in four categories. We spend time in one of four ways shown in the Time-Management Matrix.

- Quadrant II is the heart of effective management. It is the activity which we need to manage properly to avoid the crisis and convert the normal activity to a crisis.
- Bad management of time is due to:
  1. Inability to prioritise.
  2. Inability or lack of desire to organise.
  3. Lack of discipline to execute the priorities.

We must understand that when there is a big task assigned to the team leader in a team, there are several members and the activities must be divided into subactivities and all the activities should be delegated to other team members with clear authority. The team leaders should delegate to get the work done. Any great performer cannot finish the job unless he gets the necessary support from all his team members. The key to effective time management is delegation. Norman Vincent has devised a very simple formula to manage time well, he asks his readers to repeat every now and then the simple sentences, 'There is ————Plenty ——of —Time. There is —— ———Plenty ——of —Time. There is ————Plenty — —of —Time. There is ————Plenty ——of —Time.'

Case Study I

Madhu Rane, 29, is an executive secretary to Mr Iyer, Director of a leading multi-national bank in Delhi. She is the key resource person in the office of the Director; she is the only person in the corporate office of the bank to handle all sensitive investment meetings with clients and organise documents for such meetings. She has a lot of difficulty in the way in which she manages her time. The continuous pressure to meet the deadlines and being on her toes starts to reflect on her physique. Her time scheduling is not so good now. She is always under pressure to deliver and it has started telling on her health. She has been nominated by her Director to attend a time management workshop but the gains are very short lived.

The workshop she attends is on time management, she is taught how to structure time, how to differentiate between high priority and low priority activities, recognise time wasters and schedule the day to pack in more activities. The course did not have much on behavioural issues that affect time management. The crucial issues remained unaddressed. She went to a behavioural expert. He had a few self-assessment questions for her.

- Are you a chronic procrastinator?
- Do you give a lot of importance to relationships?
- What is your leadership style?
- How do you delegate?

All these activities contribute to how you manage your 24 hours. The behavioural expert suggested that she must first address these and then relate them to her problems with managing time. The change in attitude of Madhu proved to be very useful and she is a much better organised person now.

Questions:

1. Which one is more important–stress management or time management?
2. Why could Madhu not cope with the stress?

12

Manage the Complexes

What are complexes in a man? *Oxford Dictionary* defines it as 'a mental problem that makes us worry a lot about it.' What is an ego of a man? It has been defined as 'the opinion of a person for his own self'. It also means that we must have a fair and clear self-assessment. If a person has an inflated ego, he may start thinking himself superior to others. We cannot say that ego is undesirable as we all have self-interest as the top priority in life. Generally 'I' comes first whenever we try to fix some priority. The great scientist Darwin has propounded the basic natural law of survival of the fittest. As human beings we work and put all our time and energy for our own survival and for our dear ones. But is survival the only thing we would like to attain? If survival is what we need, what is the difference between a man and a street dog? The difference is his self-esteem. At times, this self-esteem takes a negative shape and the feeling of pride becomes haughtiness. This inflated ego and egocentric behaviour will land a man into a superiority complex. His behaviour will no more be guided by wisdom, but by a false sense of haughtiness. This hollow and superfluous behaviour will have an impact on his personality.

Some of us may argue that it is not wrong to protect self-interest first. A person behaves selfishly for the reason that if not he, then who else will protect his interest? Human beings are naturally egocentric and keep their interests above any one else. But if you wish to lead a dignified life in society you are required to see others also.

When we say that a person is having a complex, what does it mean? If it is regarding the superiority complex, we mean a person is suffering from a psychological disorder where a person does not consider others around him equal, as far as his education, skill, dress, riches, wealth are concerned. He will always talk to people with contempt or will treat others badly. Such people have a mental block and are not ready to accept any good suggestion and plans if they come from the persons surrounding him. It may be true for a person or it may be equally true for a nation. Say, a big nation in a UN meet does not give a hearing to a small nation, although it may be a very effective one. Due to an egocentric attitude they are deprived of more worthy suggestions.

If superiority complex is bad for a person, inferiority complex is worse. If a person treats himself below dignity, he cannot think of achieving and doing anything big. As we have discussed, a person is only as big or small by what he thinks of himself. Others may treat you badly but if you start treating your own self badly, nobody can help you. In history, we may recall the condition of Indians in South Africa before Mahatma Gandhi went there. They were humiliated and treated badly by the government and the white people of the country. Indians could not think that they were equal to the whites. If they could not even think, behaving was simply impossible.

Have you ever been bogged down by the sheer influence of riches, expensive clothes, heavy jewellery or big cars? It is a great strength in your personality if you are not influenced by the big brother attitude of people who have more wealth. The personality of a person is at test when he is dealing with someone more powerful and rich. You must give due respect and should not behave defiantly with them, but bowing down and losing your dignity is certainly nor desirous of any human being. If you show your weakness and allow others to take a ride on your pride, you are a weak person suffering from complexes. It is foolish to be adamant and hostile towards persons who are higher in social status. Rather it is advisable to take them as an example for you to try and get more and to reach the positions they are in.

The mantra to fight the complexes is to think that the most powerful in this universe is God. He has only given a small portion or part of a very big chunk that he has, to the richest individual on earth. The riches and wealth of an individual is the worst of all that he could have given. If you are lucky, God would have blessed you with wealth; if you are luckier, He would have given you good health and no physical pain; if you are the luckiest person in the world, then God would have given you peace of mind that you cannot get unless you are blessed with it. There was a very correct version of what money can buy for you by a famous Indian Guru. He asked three questions:

1. Can money buy a home? No! It can only buy a nice beautiful house.
2. Can money buy you hunger? No! It can only buy you food to eat.
3. Can money buy you education? Of course not! It can only buy you books.

Riches must never influence us, it is one thing which changes hands in no time and will always like to travel to a person who has wisdom, than to a person who is a fool. Therefore, respect knowledge and never suffer from complexes if you do not have sufficient material wealth compared to people around you.

There are many ways in which a person can cope with the problem of complexes or self-doubting attitude in him but I shall tell you the easy solutions suggested by Norman Vincent Peale, the famous author who has written the bestseller, *The Power of Positive Thinking*. In this he has prescribed ten easy steps to overcome complexes and build up your confidence.

These steps are:
1. Draw a picture of a successful person.

Everyone of us always keeps on drawing some picture of what our future will be but if we project ourself as a failure and get demoralised we will not succeed. Our action shall always try to convert these pictures in reality. Norman Peale has suggested us to draw a picture of a successful man with a dignified living. The imaginary picture when thought several times over can help a person to imprint it in his mind. Such a positive picture will take us to the road of better personality, free from all the shortcomings and lack of self-confidence.

2. Cancel your negative thoughts with a positive thought

We always keep on thinking about our future. The fear in us is due to uncertain things and doubts in our mind. These negative thoughts are the reason we are failing. To eliminate these negative thoughts we need to generate in our mind some positive and bright thoughts, which can cancel out the fear in us. Whenever these negative thoughts come in your mind start thinking of something good.

3. Identify your obstacles.

There are obstacles in your life that may be a cause of worry. If you are suffering from some ailment and you go to a doctor, he will not give you any medicine till he diagnoses you properly. Diagnosis is important for the proper treatment of the disease. Similarly, if you feel there are a few weaknesses and obstacles you need to identify and try to remove them.

4. Do not copy others blindly.

We are all unique creatures and we all have our own weaknesses and strengths. We must try to strive for something that we can do best. Why feel bad if we are not capable of doing something that others can do?

5. Get a competent counsellor to help you.

Knowing one's self is not an easy task. We start doubting our capability from childhood. The low confidence level is rooted in incidents in childhood. We feel bad about our poor competence and develop a feeling of complex. We need a counsellor who can help us know our shortcomings and the ways to overcome it.

6. Practise the sentence of telling yourself, "I can do it."

Repeat the sentence ten times daily. If you are confident that you can do it others too will start getting that feeling.

7. Make a true estimate of your ability.

The ability of a person can be physical, mental and attitudinal. It a person can make a true estimate of his physical ability, he will never feel sorry about the same. Underestimation of the ability will develop an inferiority complex.

8. God is your creator. He is for you.

When you are feeling alone and not getting any support, and everyone is on the other side of the table, you shall have one individual who will take your side, the creator of the universe. He is with you, why bother about others who are less powerful? All your inferiority complexes will vanish and you will start feeling confident.

9. Put yourself in God's hands.

Try your best, but leave the result in the hands of God. In the great Indian epic *Mahabharata*, Lord Krishna tells Arjuna that you must make all efforts and work hard and leave the results in the hands of God.

10. Remind yourself all the time that you have the energy and power of God.

When you start thinking that you do not have the last bit of energy to complete the final lap in the long distance run, the sense of desperation comes into your mind. If in that crucial moment you allow the thought of slightest complex to overrule your mind you will lose the race. At such a crucial juncture you remind yourself all the time that you have the additional energy from God to complete the last effort. The difference between a winner and a loser is the last effort, which will come from the grace of the God.

Case study I

Lokendra Pratap Singh, 26, was the only educated person in a rural village of Bihar. He had done his post-graduation in English literature. He was the son of a well-to-do peasant family who had 28 acres of land in the fertile Gangetic plain. His father was a very simple person and used to mix well with the poor villagers. But the son was an educated person; he was the first person in the village to switch to trousers and shirts. He did not like to mix with the villagers as he found them rustic and who did not know the polished language of the town. He had done computer training from one of the computer-training institutes. The course fee for the one-year training was eighty thousand rupees. His father had to sell a portion of his ancestral land to pay the fee. After completing his education he searched for a job in the city but in the prevailing job market he was unable to find a suitable one. The only job he could secure for himself was of an office assistant with a salary of a mere twelve hundred rupees. He refused to join it, as it was difficult for him to make both ends meet on this salary.

All the family members had a lot of expectations from Lokendra. Finally he had to return to his village, as there was nothing for him to do in the city. His father asked him to share his burden in cultivation and farming but he found it below his dignity to work in a farm with a post-graduate degree from a university and a computer-training institute. He told his father he could not do something which illiterate farmers were doing. He felt it would be a shame for him. He was especially not interested in wasting the expensive studies in farming. He insisted that his father sell some more land and get him a personal computer and Internet connection to set up a cyber junction in the village market so that he could earn something by providing services to the villagers.

The new venture was started with a lot of fanfare. The local MLA was invited to inaugurate the computer Internet centre. Initially it generated lot of enthusiasm in the local villagers but it was more of seeing what it is rather than using it. Lokendra thought it would be a big hit. After three months a few hundred rupees was all he could earn. This was not even sufficient to meet the rent for the phone. The project was not feasible. After six months he had to wind up the project and incurred a loss of fifty thousand rupees on selling the computer. Lokendra is a broken man now. He thinks it would have been better had he not gone to the city for education.

Questions:

1. In your opinion what is the reason for the failure of Lokendra?
2. Was the role of parents in bringing up Lokendra right?
3. Which is the place you feel should have been the right place to work for Lokendra?

Case study II

Ravi Tikku, 28, is a software professional in a leading MNC software company. He is heading a team of software developers who are responsible for implementing a package in a reputed Indian business corporate. Ravi is a very intelligent person and has proved his worth for his sharpness and wits. In the previous organisation where he worked, he was a programmer himself and used to contribute a lot, as he was independently responsible for his performance. But in this new assignment he was not finding his team members as sincere as he expected them to be. He was not finding himself in a very comfortable position to get the work done and meet the deadlines set by his Project Manager.

During one of the interactive sessions, Ravi was very critical of the performance of one of his team members Asutosh. The discussion turned into blame and counter-blame. Asutosh was very harsh and in the presence of all other superiors blamed Ravi for his autocratic attitude and hiding all important information from his team members. He was also charged with not allowing others to contribute significantly. Asutosh was ready to tender his resignation in case he was not assigned a different job in which he was not required to report to Ravi.

The company did not want to lose a good developer such as Ravi. To end the stalemate the General Manager had to intervene. He was not happy with the co-ordination efforts of Ravi and asked him to improve the situation by taking an open feedback session with his team members.

Questions:

1. What went wrong for Ravi?
2. Was he delegating to his team members properly?
3. What is your opinion to improve the effectiveness of the team?
4. Whether blaming his boss in a meeting was the right approach by Asutosh?

Case study III

Indu Jain was the youngest in a family of four sisters. The family was a traditional Jain family from Rajasthan and believed in conservative traditions. She was rebellious by nature since childhood and was very harsh on any cultural values, especially those which reminded her of Indian traditions. She did her schooling from St James School in the capital. In school, all her friends were from affluent families. She was suffering from a complex as she always wished to have all the goodies that her friend used to bring to school. Her school bag, water bottle, dress and shoes were always of cheaper quality compared to her peer group.

After her schooling she joined a college of repute in Delhi. The parents were happy that the girl was doing well in her college and was going in the right direction to achieve a good career, but little did they knew that the small girl from whom they had a lot of expectations was hardly attending any classes. She joined a group of girls who had no interest in academics. They used to spend hours sitting in canteens and bunking classes to watch movies. On one occasion, one of her neighbours saw Indu in the city cinema hall, but she convinced her parents that it was not her.

In a short span of time she was finding it difficult to meet the extra expenditure from her pocket money. She invented a very innovative way of picking the pockets of others. She started it just as fun with a few of her friends, but after some time it became a hobby. Time went by and the small Indu was a clever pickpocket on Delhi roads. She picked up the horrible habit of taking drugs and insisted on shifting to the college hostel on the basis that she found it a waste of time travelling on the college bus. Her parents thought it was good for her. But it turned out to be worse.

One day Jain was informed that his daughter was in the police lock-up at Kotwali Thana. It was a shock for him, but he had little choice and arranged for her bail. She is now a drug addict, suffering from mental dysfunction. She is undergoing anti-drug treatment in a hospital in

Dehradun. Parents and family members are praying to God for her normal recovery.

Questions:

1. Was it a matter of social complex that turned Indu rebellious?
2. Do you find it justified for her parents in sending her to a school not within their means?
3. How do you rate Indu's development as a young woman? What key actions could she have taken to avoid such an embarrassment for her and her family?

Section II
POSITIVE ATTITUDE

13

Positive Attitude Towards Life

Attitude is defined as 'the way a person feels, thinks and behaves towards a particular issue.' In the modern management theory behavioural scientists have defined it as the 'Mental-Box', which helps to show a person a particular situation in a specific frame of mind. Example: A thirsty person visit your house and you offer him a glass half-filled with water. If he has a positive attitude he will see the glass as half-filed, but if he is a person with a negative attitude, he will see it as half empty.

Can you answer a very simple question that why only a few people out of millions succeed? The answer is simple—the winner is one who has a positive attitude, self-belief and the determination to succeed. If you prioritise, the single most important factor which is the cause of success and failure is your Attitude towards what you are doing.

> 'You may be disappointed if you fail, but you are doomed if you don't try.'
>
> —Beverly Sills, American star.

Let us think in this way. The most competent striker of soccer, Ronaldo, is at the goalmouth of the opponent team. He has tackled several of the defenders and has only the goalkeeper to beat. What is that which may convert his effort to either a goal or a miss? If he is positive in attitude and is confident in his effort he will hit the ball at the right spot. Your behaviour reflects how you think. If you have a positive attitude you will think positive and the small and petty issues will not perturb you in attaining your goals.

> 'Do what you can, with what you have, where you are.'
>
> —Theodore Roosevelt.

> 'If you don't like something, change it.
> If you can't change it, change your attitude. Don't complain.'

> 'Genius is one percent inspiration and ninety-nine percent perspiration.'
>
> —Thomas Alva Edison.

Man is very similar to a complete computer system and all the organs are like the different hardware which when assembled properly will account for the total system. The system can work to the desired effect only if we have a co-ordinated approach. The work and social environment has a great role to play in the way we think and perform.

A positive attitude and will to concentrate on the work can help you achieve great heights.

'When pain ends, gain ends too.'
—Robert Browning.

The positive thinker does not see setbacks as stumbling blocks, rather as stepping-stones. The art of dealing with a fall is not to think how much it hurts but to know the reason for the fall and how to avoid it in the next attempt.

The next question that people ask is whether people are born with a positive attitude or is it developed over time? If we develop it, what are the factors which account for positive attitude? The attitude of a person generally takes shape in the formative stages of life. The way we see the environment around us—our family, school, society, media, television, political, religious and cultural backgrounds of the country, all have its share of impact during the formation stage. Can we not justify the hardworking and sincere attitude of the Japanese as a work culture consequent to their destruction in the Second World War?

If the environment of the person is so important to develop the attitude, let us review the environment we are in. It is very difficult to think positive in an environment of negative people and culture. In a destructive, barbaric and inhuman Taliban regime, can you expect someone to think positive in advancing the nation towards growth and prosperity? We must plan to leave such a negative environment for the sake of preserving and shaping positive thoughts.

> 'One machine can do the work of 50 ordinary men.
> No machine can do the work of one motivated extraordinary man.'
>
> —an unknown wise man.

What are the personality traits of people with positive attitude, and how to recognise people with positive attitude? It is very easy; they are humble, caring, confident and patient. They are raring to perform. The expectation level of such people is very high. A person of such traits is welcome in all situations, conditions and environment. He changes the scenario wherever he goes and in the grimmest of the situation he can laugh, as he knows the tragedy has already occurred and the future is always better. There are several great advantages of becoming a positive thinker. It enhances productivity, it encourages teamwork, the working environment improves, it helps in improving quality of work as well as relationship, the positive attitude also helps to reduce tensions, stress, fosters trust and finally the positive thinker is a pleasing personality. Negative thoughts in our mind give rise to animosity, ill health, bitterness and resentment. The negative thinker spoils not only himself but also the entire environment. In the life of a negative thinker, all important relationships are at stake.

If we know that negative attitude is so bad for all of us then why are we not changing our attitude! The answer is very simple. We as a part of nature always try to resist change. Any change, whether it is good or bad, is not acceptable to us. The first thing we try is to return to our natural state, of which we are habituated.

> 'No one can persuade another to change, each of us guards a gate of change that can only be opened from the inside. We can't open the gate of other person either by argument or by emotional appeal.'
>
> —Marilyn Ferguson.

The persons who are negative thinkers always try to find fault with others and the system. These critics are always there to see the negative side of the story. When the health is good they would like to find out what will happen if they become sick, when they are well-off they would try to visualise themselves as if they do not have anything. They are sadists and spend their whole life complaining and screaming at others.

I remember one incident in our office when one of our senior executives Mr Chakravorty bought a car of the latest model from the market. The looks were great and so were its features. Mr Chakravorty invited all of us for a ride. The car had extraordinary pick-up and speed. After a fantastic drive we returned to our office. Finally, Mr Chakravorty asked my friend Bose how he found the car. We knew Bose was a great critic who could hardly find anything praiseworthy. He said the car could hardly cross the speed limit of 160Kmph. We were bemused, for we all know roads in Kolkata can hardly afford a speed of 50Kmph.

The person who has a positive attitude will remain a positive thinker even if he is protesting against something. It is a state of mind. It will reflect in all his actions. A person cannot be a positive thinker on a few issues and behave negatively on others.

Kill negative thoughts

In every person's life there are periods when negative thoughts come to mind. The fear of failing and not doing well is one such thought. It is important to overcome these negative thoughts. There are many ways to keep these negative thoughts away from our minds. The worry-breaking formula can be listed below:

- Stop worrying. Whenever you are surrounded by worries, start thinking about something good and positive. Either positive or negative can stay in your mind at one point of time.
- Never participate in worrying conversations. It will always affect you. Try to avoid such groups, talk positive and take initiative in talking positive. There are people who are always worried and blame the system for their failures. Have you not heard stories from such negative talkers that law and order is poor, there is corruption in high places, the education system is pathetic, the government is not giving due attention to health and public welfare. In the morning newspaper they search for stories of gloom anywhere in the world and enjoy sharing it with the 'Gloom Club'.
- Cultivate friendship with people who have faith and hope that the world is a good place to live.
- Help others to come out of their worry habits. It will give you confidence to think positive.
- Convince yourself that the whole world will be with you to support you. The belief in God will give you

immense strength to realise that when the Energy, which created you, is with you, you are not alone.

How to Think Positive

Believe in yourself:

Have faith in your abilities. Without reasonable confidence in your own powers you cannot be successful or happy.

A peaceful mind generates power:

'A mind full of peace' is what we would all like to attain in our life and this is the basic requirement of a positive and fruitful attitude in our life. The other cryptic phrase to be avoided is, 'an ear full of trouble'. Life will be difficult and full of negative feelings if we allow negative feelings to rule our mind. We must generate the energy we need for performing well to form a successful personality.

Stop fuming and fretting:

Negative feelings start with anger. We show these feelings with expressions such as fuming and fretting. There are many people who try to grab any opportunity to shout at someone who is weak. Shouting and fuming generate negative energy and negative feeling. Practise self-restraint in shouting at someone else's fault. This will be the beginning for you to start thinking positive.

Hope for the best:

We can change our negative attitude towards life if we expect that we have seen the worst days of our life and better days are coming.

Inflow of new thoughts can remake you:

Change is what makes life charming. The new thoughts can give us fresh energy to our mind to bring positive thoughts for doing something constructive. We must always encourage fresh and new ideas.

Healing touch of positive thinking:

It is proved by medical science that a patient who has the confidence and self-belief of getting well soon is cured soon, whereas a patient who has negative thoughts takes long time to recover from any critical illness. Positive thoughts also help our glands to secrete antibodies and help us recover soon from ailments. Thus, attitudes can kill you or can give you a life full of joy.

Example: If you recall the accident of the greatest film personality in India, Amitabh Bachchan, who was badly injured on the sets of a film in Banglore. Nobody, including the doctors, had the faith that he would survive the fatal injuries inside his stomach. But strong will and positive thoughts miraculously cured Amitabh. The strong positive thoughts combined with prayers worked well for him.

Focus on your Strength:

Each and every one of us is born with some unique qualities. Some have memory, others have muscle, some have artistic flavour in whatever they do, some are tall, some are small but swift, some are beautiful and others may be having the best voice. It is we who do not recognise our qualities and try to go by the standards of others. Many people recognise their strengths at an early age and cultivate it to great heights. But such successful people are not many; losers keep on counting their limitations and curse their surroundings. Like a management consultant who undertakes the SWOT (Strength, Weakness, Opportunity and Threat) analysis for the company, each one of us at regular intervals of time, should try to find out the weaknesses we have and work in the areas of our strength. If Sachin Tendulkar is the greatest cricketer in the world, the reason is that, in spite of his short height, he could identify at an early age his artistic touch and the power he had in his wrist. He recognised his strength, fine-tuned it with hard work and dedication and the result is clear to the world.

We need to see what the great personalities have to say about the traits which can lead you to victory in life. The elements of self-confidence, strong will and determination have always superseded other individual capabilities when it comes to the situation of win or loose in life.

'If you don't have confidence, you will always find a way not to win.'
—Carl Lewis, Olympic track Star.

'I don't know the key to success, but the key to failure is trying to please everyone.'
—Bill Cosby, American actor.

Case Study I

Anil Ramani, 28, was the son of Atmaram, a school teacher, in a small town near Delhi. He lived there with his wife and four children; he did not get sufficient wages to lead a comfortable life. But he raised his son to be an engineer from IIT, Delhi and also to complete his MBA from FMS, Delhi. The whole family was pinning their hopes on a change in their fortune with Anil's success as a young marketing executive in a MNC firm in Gurgaon. The young Anil had a very simple lifestyle. He was always at the receiving end for his simple dressings sense. The young man was a bit shy and not comfortable with his peers from the opposite sex. He was not very comfortable with urban colloquial English though he was very good in the language. His problem was in verbal communication.

In his job he was to report to Mr Chadha, Regional Manager. A not-so-well-qualified person, but Mr Chadha was a hi-flier as far as verbal communication was concerned. The two persons had totally different ways of looking at things. One was meticulous and systematic whereas the other was an impressive person at first sight. Chadha found him a misfit in the marketing job from day one. It was very difficult for Anil to prove himself in a situation where he was not allowed to work freely. There was a serious misunderstanding between the two. Chadha went to the VP, Marketing, and said he did not want Anil on his team. For Anil the job was important for the survival of his family.

Anil became arrogant and started misbehaving with his subordinates to vent out his frustration. He thought assertiveness could be expressed in anger. Slowly, his peers and subordinates started avoiding him. Now he is a dejected person under tremendous pressure to save his job.

Questions:

1. Why do you think Anil failed?
2. Has he applied his relationship with the persons in the group properly?
3. State the reasons why Anil was not performing well.
4. How was his Manager's behaviour affecting the performance level?
5. What steps should Anil take for the transformation?

Case study II

Michael D'souza was the youngest of four sons of the mill supervisor in a small suburban town of Mumbai. He did excellently in school level athletics. But his father was always concerned for his performance in academics and was worried that in case he does not perform well in class it will be difficult for him to find a suitable job for his career. One day Michael came overjoyed with the news that he has been selected as a sprint runner to represent the zonal school team. He was expecting his parents also to encourage him with appreciation. But to his surprise his father was not at all happy with the news. He was worried that he would miss many important days of class.

D'souza did not dare to ask his father for the new sprint runner kit, which would cost two thousand rupees. The boy was sad now and was wondering if it was possible for him to attend the training camp. The unkind words from his father caused the low motivation level. But he had his strong determination to excel in this arena and finally achieve something great for his parents.

Without telling his father, he applied for a scholarship with the Tata-Foundation and practised when he got time. After fifteen days he got a positive response from the academy. He discussed the prospect with his sports teacher and in spite of his father's unwillingness, joined the academy. The academy gave him opportunity to practice and learn the art of winning tough competitions. The training by a national coach resulted in positive change in the stamina of young D'souza. He was shaping well for the forthcoming All India University Competition. In the competition D'souza was victorious and clocked a timing which was better than the national record. The record breaking timing drew the attention of the Sports Authority of India. The skills of D'souza got the recognition he wanted most. The Asian Track and Field event in Jakarta saw a new star in Michael.

Questions:

1. Was overlooking his studies right on the part of Michael?
2. Was the strength of Michael identified correctly?
3. What contributed to the success of Michael the most, will power or attitude?
4. Was his parents' role in shaping his future right?

14

Dare to Think Big and Win

We must believe that much more can be achieved in life if we dare to take that first step, by building our confidence and self esteem. APJ Abdul Kalam, famous nuclear scientist and President of India has very correctly said that 'Dream, dream and dream. Think, think and think and put that thought in action, action and action.'

Sow a Thought
↓
Reap an Action
↓
Sow an Action
↓
Reap a Habit
↓
Sow a Habit
↓
Reap a Destiny

'Begin with the end in mind', Stephen Covey has correctly said. It's incredibly easy to get yourself caught in an activity trap. You ask any of your friends, 'what you doing today evening?' The reply most of the time will be, they are very busy. If you ask very specifically, 'what for are you busy?' They can further tell that they are busy in some activity. In the busy life, people are caught up in an activity trap. Everybody is working hard and harder to climb the ladder of success, but the ladder should be leaning against the right wall. There is every possibility that those who are busy are so without being very effective. People often find themselves achieving victories that are empty. The final aim of what they try for is different from what they achieve. People generally compromise on many things, which are far more valuable to them than what they achieve. I have come across several professional experts from the field of academics, doctors, lawyers, business professionals and technical people. Many of them struggle to achieve a higher income, more recognition or better professional competence. But after a few years they find that their drive to achieve that goal blinded them to things which really mattered the most to them, and now they are gone.

> Watch your thoughts; they become words
> Watch your words; they become habits
> Watch your habits; they become characters
> Watch your character; they become destiny.

Example: Kiran Bedi, the first woman IPS officer in the country when inducted into the police force, dominated by males, was looked upon as a soft, good looking girl (*chokri*) not capable of delivering the hard duty demanded by such a job. She was asked to rescue seventeen women in a Delhi suburb. When the males did not have the courage to enter the burning house, the young lady officer established herself by leading from the front and jumping into the fire-blazed entrance. The incident was enough to transform the image of a *chokri* into a strong officer. The officer in her blossomed into a great human being when she helped improve the lives of inmates in the largest jail in India, the Tihar Jail. That was of course not considered a part of any officer's job. The effort was her own larger aim, which was good enough to win her the Magsasay award. The young Kiran was a girl when she joined, became a madam due to her sincerity, and earned the reputation of the best officer due to her big dreams to serve humanity. Now she is the *Sir jee* in the police force.

> 'Most of the important things in the world have been accomplished by people who have kept on trying when there seemed to be no hope at all.'
> —Dale Carnegie.

A real achiever of success is one who knows what is important to him. He can manage each day as per what really matters most to him. You need to define the success you want. Each individual has a different definition and thought for success. It's always a possibility that fame, achievement, money or some other item, which we strive so hard to attain, are not what we consider as our success path. One man asked another on the death of a mutual friend, 'How much did he leave?' His friend responded, 'He left it all'.

> 'It must be born in mind that the tragedy of life does not lie in not reaching your goal. The tragedy lies in having no goal to reach. It isn't a calamity to die with dreams unfulfilled, but it is a calamity not to dream. It is not a disaster to be unable to capture your ideal, but it is a disaster to have no ideal to capture. It is not a disgrace not to reach the stars, but it is a disgrace to have no stars to reach.'
>
> —Benjamin Mays.

We must always try to see the better side of life and hope for the better. It is rightly said that we must hope for the best and prepare for the worst. The persons who are optimistic, get courage and strength from all quarters.

> 'Do not pray for easy life, pray to be a stronger man,
> Pray for powers equal to the tasks,
> Then the doing of your work shall be no miracle,
> But you shall be a miracle.'
>
> —Phillip Brooks.

Section III

CHARACTER TRAITS

16

Career Planning

It is human nature to expect growth and development. In an environment of change, a person as an individual or working in a company must always strive to do better and grow. The best of salary and the best of perks cannot give any morale boost if career progression and planning is not taken care of properly. As observed by John Leach, it is ironical that what is most precious to the individual so far as work is concerned, is career. But it is given the least attention by the organisation.

Unskilled worker → Skilled worker → Supervisor → Team leader
Engineer → Asstt. Manager → Dy. Manager → Manager
General manager → Vice President → Chairman

What is the need of a career plan

Career Planning essentially means helping the employees to plan their career in terms of their capabilities in the to follow as principles in life. Give a few minutes to your self and try to think if at all we are on the right path. Let me start the chapter with the hard work and the sacrifice of a few great persons in history to keep their character traits at high standards.

Mohandas as he was known in his childhood, was a staunch supporter of truth and honesty. He attended a school in a small town of Gujarat. Once the Inspector of Schools was scheduled to inspect. Everybody was very alert and the headmaster was especially keen to present a better image of the school. The Inspector went to the class in which Mohandas was a student. To ascertain the knowledge of the students, he gave them a few dictations. The spelling Mohandas wrote was not right, the teacher was standing in front of him. He hinted to Mohandas to copy the right one from the boy next to him. Mohandas refused to budge knowing well that the teacher would not spare him for his refusal once the Inspector left the class. This was an ordinary incident but the foundation that was based on such truth and honesty was good enough to make Gandhi out of the little boy. He deserved to become the Father of the Nation.

Greatest of all American Presidents, Abraham Lincoln, hailed from a very poor family. He did all petty works like feeding animals, harvesting crops, planting, and chopping trees to earn enough to go to school. But he had a clear aim. He did not have money to buy books; he borrowed and copied them in the candlelight. At the age of 21 he started his career as a mailman in a village. But Lincoln's peculiar ambition led him to become a reputed lawyer, and eventually the president of USA. Not many people believed he would achieve either of his goals. He had far-fetched peculiar ambition, which he strived for and succeeded.

Ethics—Do not compromise on this.

During the devastating earthquake in Kobe, Japan, an American newscaster saw a Japanese woman selling flashlights and batteries in a small makeshift shop, which was made up of wooden boxes. There was a great demand for batteries and flashlight torches as there was no electricity. The newscaster went to the lady and asked why she was not selling the essential items for more than the regular price. The woman answered, 'Why would I want to profit from someone else's suffering?' These are the ethical values of citizens of a great country like Japan.

Character Ethics: Character ethics has nine dimensions as suggested by Behavioural Scientists. In the initial years, character ethics was considered the foundation of success. The important issues were:

1. *Integrity*: The Oxford Dictionary defines it as honesty, the oneness of honest approach, which cannot be disintegrated.
2. *Humility*: Person having a low opinion of one's importance, less proud.
3. *Fidelity*: The faithfulness and loyalty of a person.
4. *Temperance*: It is the quality of self-restraint, moderation, and total abstinence from alcohol.
5. *Courage*: It is the ability to control fear when facing danger or pain.

6. *Justice*: It is the quality of a person of being fair or reasonable.
7. *Patience*: It is the ability of calm tolerance.
8. *Simplicity*: It is the quality of a man who is not showy, proud or extravagant.
9. *Modesty*: Not behaving boastfully and avoiding indecency.

Covey has said that character ethics teach that there are basic principles of effective living and that people can only experience true success and enduring happiness as they learn and integrate these principles into their character. People like Covey, Gandhi and Lincoln are examples of strong followers of character ethics.

Followers of character ethics acknowledge character as the main ingredient of success. Personality ethics believers recognise it as only the foundation, and believe that other issues such as interpersonal relationship, communication skills and positive attitude play a more important role in achieving success.

They have identified four basic qualities or traits:
- **Character**
- **Competence**
- **Integrity**
- **Acceptance**

Character: For any relationship to prosper, character is the prime quality, which a man must possess. A person may have all the good qualities in him. But without character, he cannot be trusted and therefore can never ever build a sound platform of relationship. A fox is cunning by character and will behave so when it gets an opportunity even with the best of friends. It is character that communicates most eloquently. Generally to improve a relationship a person uses human influence, strategies and tactics to get people to do what he wants, to motivate them, to influence them to work better, to like him and each other without focusing on character building which is not going to last long. The flawed character marked with insincerity in a relationship cannot be successful. Duplicity in a relationship will breed distrust and the best of human relationship technique will be taken as manipulative techniques. The best example is the process of farming. Farm is a natural system. The price must be paid and the process followed. You always reap what you sow: 'There is no shortcut.' The most modern invention of man that has changed human life and his way of thinking, that is computers, also could not change this natural law, i.e. 'Garbage In, Garbage Out'.

About the foundation of character and what makes it, William George Jordan narrated it very correctly as, 'Into the hands of every individual is given a marvellous power for good or evil—the silent unconscious, unseen influence of his life. This is simply the constant radiation of what man really is, not what he pretends to be.' An old tiger promising nice and polished behaviour to its prey can hardly create a sense of trustworthy relationship.

Duplicity in behaviour and double standards in dealing with people cannot be sustained forever. When such dubious behaviour is exposed, the people around will never forgive you . No man in this world ever wants to be cheated and the worst wounds a person can inflict on others is by cheating. Character is one trait, which comes to its own, when a person is at ease and not under any pressure to buckle.

Out of all the major personality traits of a man the most difficult to change is character building. Character is the structure of the building and is developed on several layers of time-tested concrete. The character of a man comes to its fore at times of distress. People generally resort to unfair and easy path at the time of odds against him. The real test of a person's character is when everything is adverse to him, including his own relatives not willing to come forward for any help. But it is equally true that people who have experienced such kind of trauma with grace, stand in high esteem of those around him. It is at a time when loneliness is the only companion of a man with hurdles around, that the true strong character comes out to overcome the problems.

Competence: It comes when a person has the right kind of ability complemented with attitude to serve. The best of knowledge and skills without the right kind of attitude does not make a man competent.

'If we cannot believe in ourselves, who else will.' There is only one winner amongst several contenders having the same strength, same calibre and skills. A loser gives up the race before it starts, thinking that it cannot be won. I know many of my friends, who did well during their school days. Nobody had any doubts about their competence. But to tell my readers, very few of them have really achieved anything to mention about afterwards. The reason for their losing before they started playing was complacency. Competence can bring success if, and only if the person is strong and resolute. You yourself should be convinced first and then only can you cross the hurdles.

The famous book 'Think and Grow Rich' by Napoleon Hill has taught an invaluable lesson that one should not give up the fight on the ground that one would loose. There are several people in our society who are symbols of gloom and who advise not to venture in any new field. They will never try anything new themselves nor allow others to think or try something new. Their plea for not venturing into something new may be one of the following:

- It has been attempted before but without success.
- It is a risky proposition.
- What society will say; they will not accept it.
- It goes against government policy.
- I do not have time to try something new.

Next time when you are trying one of the excuses mentioned above you must know in which category you are. You are the best judge.

Acceptance: If we want to have a good relationship we must know the importance of accepting each other with all the plus and minus points we have. Changing a person as per your own requirement will always create a strained relationship.

Integrity: Integrity is based on the principle of fairness, the principle which gives birth to equity and justice. No example can be better than the sense of fairness prevailing in children. Even in adverse conditions the definition of fairness remains the same. **Steven Covey** has showed personal integrity as the basis of creating goodwill, which generates trust. Lack of integrity can undermine any effort to create trust in relationships. Even people who seek to understand, remember the little things, keep their promises, clarify and fulfil expectations, fail to build a relationship because they are inwardly duplicitous. Integrity is more than honesty.

Honesty in simple words is telling the truth, or in other words, is conforming our words to reality. Integrity is conforming reality to our words or in other words keeping promises and fulfilling the expectations.

One of the best ways to explain integrity is to be loyal to those who are not present. In doing so we build the trust of those who are present. When you defend those who are absent you retain the trust of those who are present. Never sweet-talk in somebody's face and bad mouth behind his back. That's the essence of duplicity.

Section IV

ACTION PLAN

15

Ethics & Values

When we talk about personality many of you will be wondering why the author is so keen to tell us the character traits which most of us already know. Let me tell you that there is a great need to have a strong foundation to any big structure. Never forget that the height of the building we see is only the visible half. The great monuments which are there for hundreds of years is due to the bottom half of their strong foundation. If you want to develop your personality, you are also required to give a fresh look to your character. We discussed in detail the behavioural traits of a good personality, but to complement that discussion, we shall discuss the basic character traits. Please do not skip this step.

When we were small, and our teachers and parents told what the character of a great man should be, we used to think of all these traits as very simple, nothing difficult context of organisational needs. It is described as devising an organisational system of career movement and growth opportunities. A person joins an organisation and grows in the organisation till he retires. It is rightly said that an organisation will gain strength and vitality only when its employees are convinced that they will also stand to gain thereby, not only in financial and other tangible terms, but also emotionally and mentally and that they will ascend the Maslow's scale. One way to achieve is by proper career planning. Career planning synergises and harmonises the individual's needs with the need of the organisation which will not only help the fulfillment of individual aspirations of an employee but also improve the organisation's effectiveness. In a company an employee's career graph is depicted in the above flow chart.

Career planning must include:

1. Assessment of occupational and career choice.
2. Personnel assessment.
3. Annual appraisal and development programme.

We need to understand whose responsibility it is to plan a career. Is it the companies' HR department who need to work for career planning or an individual employee or a student who must do it? Basically, it is the responsibility of an individual. But in an organisation, to retain and encourage the potential of the employees, it is also a present trend to plan the career and progression of their employees to derive the maximum benefit for the organisation.

Procedure of career planning

For students it is important to plan their career. Unless we know what we want to achieve, we cannot achieve it. We can say that there are two components of career planning and development:

Career development programme consists of three activities, namely, the facilitating of a student to assess his own career needs, publicity by institutions to notify career growth and opportunity for students, or finding ways for an institute to bridge the gap between opportunity and career.

Career planning activity. These are the activities to facilitate the process of career planning:

- **Internal Career Assessment:** The best person to assess the need of a career and growth is the person himself. But a counsellor can always help to assess the need in a better way. He can provide the necessary information and help in the assessment of capability, attitude and performance level in work.
- **Career Opportunities:** Based on the attitude, competence and performance level, each individual has to chart a road map for career growth. The counsellor or the institute can assist in informing the career opportunities to the students.

The assessment of gap between need and opportunity
When students or employees have assessed their

respective needs and have become aware of their career plans the next step is to find ways to bridge the gap between the opportunity and the needs.

Limitations of career planning

It seems very fascinating to hear that career planning is the easy way to reach the destination in your career. There are several positive factors why an individual as well as institutions must plan the career. But at the same time there are many points, which does not allow career planning to succeed all the time.

- In India economic and social conditions are changing fast, therefore career plans beyond ten years are not generally practical.
- Career planning is only suitable in a large institution, organisation, and city where there is plenty of opportunity for growth and progression.
- It cannot be perfectly applicable in the environment where there are a large number of people competing for very few openings.
- Family owned business dominates Indian industry and such socio-economic environment affects career plans.
- In our environment, political interference, nepotism, favouritism are predominant in progress and promotions.

17

How to Write an Impressive Résumé

Résumé is a piece of paper, which goes to a prospective employer before you can reach there. It is a document that tells about you to the employer/consultant. A résumé must reflect your personality in a holistic manner. We must know what must be covered in a résumé and the information which may be avoided, what is the optimum size of a résumé, what should be the font size, etc.

The objective of preparing a well written résumé is to get the attention of the employer at the first place. In fiercely fought competition, it must have a different approach. These days, many employers make first level selection by screening the résumés. This stage is not in control of your other abilities as the résumé is the source of information for the HR consultant. Therefore even if you have any edge over others, you may lose the race in the very beginning if the résumé does not have the right presentation.

The résumé must have the following:

1. **The size of résumé:** The résumé should have an optimum size of not more than two A-4 size papers. The size must be enough to have the information required for the post you have applied for. The experience and other details must not be exhaustive. Résumés written in more than two pages are a waste as consultants hardly have the time to read the extra pages and the annexure you have attached to it.
2. **The font in the résumé:** The font in the MS-Word format should be New Times Roman in 12 size. The other artistic fonts used for the résumé do not go well with the employer. It shows unprofessional presentation and attitude. The résumé should be structured such that it also indicates your personality.
3. **Tell the facts, do not exaggerate:** The person who will scrutinise your CV is experienced and must have seen several hundred such CVs prior to this. You are fooling yourself, if you hide some information or exaggerate your achievements. It is very easy on the part of an experienced consultant to assess the facts.
4. **Tailor make your CV:** In most cases people prepare the CV once, get it laser printed and send copies to vacant positions which appear on the net/newspapers. But just imagine if someone serves you rice and sambar for breakfast even if he has a choice of idli to eat. The ingredients of rice and idli may be the same but they fit in for different requirements at different times of the day. Similarly, if a company is looking for a

particular post, you need to present yourself as per the company needs.
5. **Synopsis of your suitability:** We all cover the academic qualifications, extra curricular activities, experiences, hobbies, etc. in our CVs. But what can separate the men from boys is the clearly spelled synopsis of what makes you suitable for the post. The synopsis has to be covered in a brief paragraph stating your strength, which can fulfil the requirement of the post you have applied for.
6. **Covering letter:** The covering letter is required to be polite, referring to the source of information about the vacant position. The letter must not have the details of your bio-data as they are not recorded in offices. You must not give too much emphasis on your need of the job, rather the way the company would benefit from your service to the organisation.

Decoding the advertisement requirements

It is important to know the requirement of the vacant position in the company. The companies generally use some of the common jargons, which convey certain messages. We need to understand these messages prior to taking up the assignment.

Some of the HR consultants have very aptly said that, 'The job advertisement conceals as much as they reveal.' When you are scanning an advertisement you will find some of the jargon, such as *dynamic* and *persons who can take initiative, flexible,* etc. Let us find out what these jargons should mean to an applicant.

The first thing a person must do after seeing the advertisement is to visit the website of the company, contact through the telephone number, get the information you feel necessary to understand the job profile. Let us find out the actual meaning of few of the jargons commonly used.

- **Need to take initiative:** In such a situation, the company may need a person who will need little support to execute the project. He is required to have the urge and fire in his belly. The person needed for such positions must be energetic, opportunity-grabbing and raring to go. You must have the drive to take an initiative on your own accord.
- **Proven track record:** In such cases people are interested to see the work achievement in terms of facts and actual figures. Nobody generally is interested to know the name of the project or products you have dealt with, they may be interested to see what you did there.
- **Need a sense of humour:** Gone are the days when people used to expect an officer to be reserved, tight-lipped and talk only business. With the trend changing fast, an executive is required to behave in a more sensible way and can share lighter moments with his team. The working environment is supposed to be enjoyable. Of course he is not required to be cracking jokes but he certainly should not be grim-faced.

- **Quick learner:** In the fast world of today one does not have much time to learn on the job. He is required to be sufficiently capable to start within a fortnight. He cannot expect that the company will provide him long duration in-house training before assigning the job.
- **Dynamic individual:** As minute division of labour has been done away with, companies are trying to seek people who can change positions in their jobs pretty fast. Most of the MNCs do need such people. Therefore the dynamics of the individual must match the dynamics of the company.
- **Demanding environment:** The policy of the new generation companies is very simple, keep less people and pay them better. If they are motivated they can take up more responsibility. It is always better to have few motivated individuals rather than a host of lazy, unmotivated workers. Therefore if a company is looking for a demanding environment, the company is indicating no fixed working hours and the person may have to play more than one role.
- **Play a key role:** In such cases you are supposed to be the person who will lead the team and will be responsible for its failure or success. Your leadership qualities and the ability to get work done will be the requirement of the job.
- **A promising future:** When the company is not too sure of its future they may use these kinds of jargons. The companies must have clear strategies

and goals, which they want to achieve. Anything very unclear and vague can be attractive but not always good. The experience of the best of the brains losing a few of their best years in dot.coms is still fresh in our memory.

- **Fresh culture and exciting strategy:** In traditional Indian society where every change takes a long period to implement, positive change in our work culture is always welcome. But do not forget that structural reforms in UK were completed in two years whereas we, after ten years of reforms have crossed very few hurdles.
- **Attractive salary and benefit packages:** The company is not so sure about what the right salary will be. They would like to judge an individual on a case-to-case basis and will take a decision based on the suitability of the candidate.

Common pitfalls in writing a CV

There are many things a person must avoid when writing a CV. Let us try to find out what these irritants are.

1. Keep your résumé error free, both in terms of language and facts. The errors in your CV may make a consultant think that if you are so careless with your CV, how can you be careful about the job?
2. Give by only the relevant information about yourself. Do not write everything about your life. Nobody is interested in your personal background.

3. Uncomfortable zones must not be touched upon in a CV; similarly the glorious events in your life may not sound so glorious to the recruiter.
4. Irritants such as failure in exam, marriage or business may be left to be discussed during the interview. They should not form a part of the CV.
5. Never give wrong information.
6. Do not beat around the bush. Irrelevant information can frustrate the attempt of a recruiter to find a CV amongst a heap of CVs. Try to convince the recruiter with relevant information only.
7. Avoid flamboyant and flowery language. The sections in your CV telling about who I am what are my strengths where I would like to be in ten years, should not give the impression that the applicant is boastful of his self.
8. Do not send your photograph unless it is specifically asked for.
9. Do not touch upon unnecessary details such as reasons for leaving your last job, the details of the perks and other facilities you get in your present job, etc. These, if required, might be discussed during the interview.
10. Never send a poor quality photocopied CV, this can only give an impression that you are applying to a lot of places.
11. Family achievements and family background will unnecessarily waste precious space of your CV.

18

Power Dressing–An Investment

It is very common to hear people suggest to others to be totally altruistic and recommend that dress has hardly anything to do with success. You may find plenty of persons in this world who will suggest to you that it is your strong inner self and self-confidence that will give you the edge to win. In this respect we may sound different. The very vital tip for success, is to dress for success and do not postpone your dressing till you are successful. More than what we wear is how we wear our dress. The dresses you wear are not just a status symbol but are in the true sense your presentation of your personality.

Do you know that most of the successful people in this world had always put a lot of emphasis on their dresses? Late Indira Gandhi had a perfect dress sense and hairstyle, which was very unique. People throughout the world still remember her gorgeous saris. The former American president Bill Clinton always presented a neat and smart picture of himself and the country he represented. George Washington was very particular about his attire and the car he used. He mentioned once that with the large car he travelled, people could separate him from the crowd. President Hamid Karzai of Afghanistan is identified with impeccable and articulate dress sense not only in his country but throughout the world. All the great successful people had their own unique dress and style.

A poorly dressed person singles himself out as a failure. Why, in India there is a general perception that all the un-smart people are working in PSUs and government departments. The reason is very simple. These people consider the expenditure on proper dressing as wasteful, whereas their peers in the private sector consider it as an investment. The dress you are wearing should be tailored to your size and should not be rumpled and sweaty. We must never forget a basic human nature, that people resent sloppiness and would like to discard such people. 'The first 30 seconds of interaction with any one will create the basis for the everlasting impression of that person' – Ziglar.

Effective Dress Code: In spite of the best of intentions no one will allow a rustic looking guy with an unshaven face to enter one's office. If you cannot enter the office how can you have an impact on the person? Below are few general tips to be a winner:

- You must *plan* to win, you must prepare to win, and you must expect to win.
- Is your dress appropriate and as per the requirement of the job?

- Do you feel at home with the group in your attire?
- Will you be acceptable at the front desk?

If all the above questions are in YES then only you are right as far as your dress code is concerned. The perfect dress is not uniform for all professions. There is one area where every Management Guru will agree that the best dress a man can wear is a smile.

Dress code for interviews:

In our career, interviews are the first gates toward success. We all have to appear for some interview or the other. As soon as you enter for an interview, people on the board will try to form an opinion about you. Behavioural experts say that the first thirty seconds are most crucial. Your behaviour, postures, actions, and of course your dress, will help you to win the race in thirty seconds. The piercing eyes which act as a scanner for your behaviour would like to judge you on face value first. The mental frame of a personality is determined from his appearance and behaviour. Therefore we cannot ignore the importance of dressing when we are ready to face unknown faces in the interview board.

There may be different opinions about what should be the dress code during an interview. But one common opinion in all the viewpoints is that the dress you wear must present you as a smart and neat person. Very loose baggy dresses are taken as relaxed and casual, whereas very skin tight dresses reflect a serious type of personality. Try not to personify your self with the dress you wear.

The dress you wear must match the requirement of the job you have applied for. For a sales job you are required to be formally attired. The very commonly accepted dress during an interview should be dark colour (preferably, black or blue) formal trouser with not so many pleats, and on top of it some light colour full sleeved formal shirt without unorthodox design for men. A necktie and blue blazer can be worn as per the weather conditions. But as the weather in India is warm and humid, we can avoid wearing the blazer and tie during summer or months other than winter. A sweating candidate is always perceived as a nervous person. The dress should be complemented with hygienic care such as a clean shaven face, cut nails, trimmed and combed hair, nice polished shoe (formal black or brown shoes). If you are sneezing at a public place, use the apologetic words. Lavishly use the words for courtesy.

It is all the more important for girl candidates to care about what they wear for an interview. No one would like to see you in a dress you use for attending parties. Never use dark make-up, lots of jewellery, dark coloured printed dress and uncomfortable high heels for an interview. The dress must give you a sober but smart look. The choice of dress shall depend largely on which place you are applying at. If you are appearing for an MNC executive job your dress must be of international style, trousers and matching shirt. But for Indian companies you are well received if you wear a nice salwar-kurta or sari. It is always preferable to choose a dress which goes with your personality.

Office dress code

'When you are in Rome do what Romans do', this is a very practical approach for the office you attend. Every company and office in India will have some unwritten dress code and its own culture. If you match the requirement with the local cult, the cultural barrier will not keep you in isolation.

When you visit an office in London, you will not find any person attending office in informal wear, they all have accepted this as a part of their job. But go to any Scandinavian country such as Sweden or Norway, you will find people comfortably using a nice pair of jeans and polo shirts in the office. Indian office is a mixed culture. The office culture in metros are more inclined to international standards, but the smaller towns and rural offices still see people in very unsmart looking clothes. Invest in your dress, that will not only help you boost your career but also give you more confidence in dealing with people.

19

Develop a Hobby

We need to have a constant source of energy. This source can be the mental strength. Our physical limitation is very much affected by how we think and how we feel. If our mind tells us that we are tired, the body mechanism, the nerves and the muscles accept the fact. If your mind is interested in any activity, you can keep on doing that activity without ever feeling tired of it. Therefore it is essential for us to make our activities interesting to our mind. Persons who are energetic and full of vigour and vitality are those who get the battery regularly charged by imposing self-faith in what they are doing. The other source of this vitality and energy is proper care and nurturing the body, taking simple care of it and not abusing it. Norman Vincent has suggested the formula of 'Believe in whatever you do and say. Be enthusiastic about your convictions.' The mixing of the necessary pleasure with your activities can be achieved by developing a hobby.

Hobbies can help you to build a fine personality. We all have some time to relax. Some spend it watching TV, others spend it gossiping and some other reading books. Before we start discussing what we need to do as a hobby to improve our personality, I would like you to do a small exercise. We may spend a few minutes before we go to the next section to find out how we have spent the day in the last seven days and what was our routine.

Action I:

Take a piece of paper. Sit at a desolate and peaceful place. Spend a few minutes in recalling the way you have spent the last week. We may exclude the time we spent in doing daily work such as eating, daily hygiene, etc. List out the work you have done and how you spent your time during your leisure hours. What is generally your favourite pastime?

If you are watching too much TV and/or gossiping with your friends, it is time to reorient your thinking. Watching TV does not keep your brain in use as we only see and listen. Therefore persistent viewers become dull after a period. Similarly, gossiping with your friends always involves criticising someone. We must avoid such situations. We may categorise three types of people.

    Category I—Persons who discuss people.
    Category II—Persons who discuss events.
    Category III—Persons who discuss philosophy.

The worst of all the gossipers are the ones who discusses persons and their shortcomings. The more intellectual person will discuss an event and if you are great you will discuss philosophy. God has made us all with some shortcomings, why find it in others when there are many in our selves? Few of the good habits to be inculcated in the younger people are:

Book reading

Book reading makes you think. The more you think, the more you know how better you can do the job. Joining a good public library is the ideal way of spending your free time constructively. Never read a book for immediate gain. The knowledge you acquire never goes waste.

> 'Reading is to the mind, what exercise is to the body.'
> —Joseph Addison, English essayist and poet.

Close to nature

If nature inspires you, spending your time on your plants and pots, doing horticulture is an excellent hobby. In cities, people do not get sufficient space to pursue this hobby. But if you begin with a few pots it is good constructive work. You can find out what your talents are.

Many great people grew famous from what began as a hobby. Jagdish Chandra Bose's hobby was keeping rats, snakes and other animals in his house. He used to compare them with plants and other living bodies; this study later on made him a great scientist. Many writers like Enid Blyton wrote stories as a hobby; but soon they became great writers and people still read their books.

Case Study I

Deepa was a post-graduate student in Chennai University. She always considered that education was not her first priority. Her parents were from a famous family from Chennai. She had always done whatever she thought was interesting. Deepa took social service as her main pastime. She was greatly inspired by the great work done by Mother Teresa for the poor and helpless in Kolkata. There were many instances in which her parents also supported her to pursue extra-curricular activities. She took the initiative in forming a non-profit NGO (non governmental organisation) for social service with the help of family friends. She was spending two hours every day in organising evening adult education classes for the poor women in the nearby village.

Deepa had to compromise with her studies to pursue this hobby, but the response she got was really encouraging. Even the government was supporting her initiative with a special grant for her evening school. She took the hobby more seriously and desired to become a social worker. The long cherished dream of Deepa was fulfilled when UNESCO recognised her social welfare scheme as a unique model for semi-urban villages.

She could not complete her PG course and left it for the UNESCO Pilot project which came her way.

Questions:

1. Was the taking up of social work as hobby by Deepa a correct step?
2. To accommodate the hobby of social service, can Deepa cope with her studies too?
3. Has she achieved the final goal?

20

Importance of Fitness and Yoga

A man is just like any other machine. After using for a few years the machine needs regular maintenance, an investment which is is important as the initial one when it is bought. Similarly we do spend a lot of money, time and energy when we are in an institute to acquire knowledge, skill and competence to make a good living. But gone are the days when a doctor used to treat his patients for more than fifty years based on the knowledge he acquired during the MBBS course. With changing technology, knowledge is getting obsolete faster than ever before. Many behavioural scientists have suggested different solutions to this problem throughout the world. Professionals in America are engaged for a period of one to three years at the most. The performance and the usefulness of the person is reassessed after this period of contract. You are not allowed to relax but pressed to keep your performance at your best and try to acquire additional skills. In India too, although employees may not be prepared for such insecure working environment, but with the arrival of MNCs, the competition among executives is getting tougher. An executive is always under pressure to perform better. The great Covey has said, *'Sharpen the saw with balanced self-renewal'*.

There are phases in our life when we find that the energy level and the mental frame is not giving us enough support to take up our plans of success and achieving something big. When you buy a costly machine you do the needful planning and implementation to get maximum benefit from the investment. But after a few years, in spite of the best upkeep and maintenance, the machine will need a complete overhaul. This is the period when the owner of the machine has to rework the entire plan of giving a new lease of life to the machine.

Human body is also made up of very sophisticated and complex components. Man uses and misuses his body to a great extent. Body management is important for having a perfect body. There are many professionals who are providing detailed courses on the revival of human energy and vitality. But we would like to see what are the basics to improve our personality.

In this fast paced world, all new generation executives are under stress and strain that lead to various disorders in the human body and mind. The stress is more painful if work satisfaction is not there and an individual is not achieving higher levels of mental satisfaction. We set targets for ourselves but once they are not met, it causes immense stress. Stress can be experienced in various forms. It is an art to handle stress with tremendous care and patience.

Stress, the Greatest Danger

In this generation one of the most dangerous of all diseases is the one which we get due to stress and strain. Stress is an invisible disease that disturbs an individual's mental health in a way which also ultimately affects the physical well being. It refers to an individual's reaction to a disturbing factor in the environment. It is defined as an adaptive response to an external situation that results in physical, psychological and behavioural deviations for organisational participants.

Beehr and **Newman** have defined stress as a condition arising from the interaction of people and their jobs and are characterised by changes within people that force them to deviate from their normal functioning.

Some of the behavioural scientists have identified stress as both positive and negative. Positive stress work as a motivator since in its absence, the individual lacks the cutting edge that is necessary for peak performance. Stress can become negative when associated with heart-disease, alcoholism, drug abuse, marital breakdowns, absenteeism and a host of other social, physical, organisational and emotional problems. It is a result of excessive performance of body beyond the normal range.

Stress is the imbalance between demands made on an individual, which is generally from external sources, and the capabilities of an individual to meet those demands and his performance level. It affects all, young or old, boy or girl, urban or rural, rich or poor, educated or uneducated, servant or master. We need to take a daily exercise routine as well as yoga to come out of this stress. There are yoga gurus to tell you more on this aspect of life but in this book, which is meant to help improve your personality, we shall touch on a few of these basic steps.

1. **Physical** (exercise, nutrition, stress management) The preliminary of all renewal processes is physical improvement in a person. There have always been questions as to why there is so much importance and priority for physical renewal. The reason is simple, but clear. The physique of a person can influence other people.
2. **Mental** (reading, visualising, planning, writing)
3. **Spiritual** (value clarification, commitment, study, meditation)
4. **Social/Emotional** (service empathy, synergy, intrinsic security)

Daily Exercise

Without taking any extra time you can improve your mind and body by developing the following habits in a routined way:

1. Press both hands with the fingertips. Clap and rub your hands and rub your face, neck, chest and abdomen with your hands and come to your knees and massage.
2. **Vajrasana:** Sit on feet, legs bent backward for 4-5 minutes, 2-3 times a day. Beneficial after meals, aids gastric system.

3. **Makrasana:** Lie flat on stomach, then raise torso on folded hands (TV Watching Position)—at least 10 minutes per day—2 times.
4. **Agnisar:** Hold your breath and pump your abdomen repeatedly. Start with 4-5 times and then slowly increase the exercise.

Warm up Exercise

Eyes Exercise—(1) Close eyes (softly), (2) Open-Close tight, (3) Look up and down while holding the head straight, and then sideways, concentrating on the movement of the right hand thumb. Pressure—(1) Pinch eyebrows (2) Press and rotate eye corner, (3) Press and rotate cheek bones, (4) Caress eyebrows and cheek bones. (4-5 times)

Neck Exercise—Press neck back while inhaling and back slowly while exhaling. Press forehead with both palms while inhaling and hold. Press neck forward with hands while applying reverse pressure by neck. Massage back of neck (rotation). (4-5 times)

Shoulder Exercises—Rotate both shoulders with hands folded, fingers touching shoulders—clock wise and anticlockwise. Press shoulder back while inhaling—hold and then bring forward while exhaling and touch elbows in front.

Leg Exercise—Lie flat on back, straighten legs and rotate ankle back and forward and then in circular motion. Knees to remain tight in backward press only.

ASANAS

Yogmudrasana—While in Vajrasana hold hands at the

back and bend forward slowly while exhaling. Remain in the position for sometime and then return to Vajrasana while inhaling. To be done on an empty stomach or 3 hours after meal. (5-6 times. People with lower back problem to avoid).

Bhujangasana—Lie flat on stomach, hands folded and kept by the side and raise torso while inhaling, hold and then down while exhaling. To be done on an empty stomach. (5-6 times)

Salabhasana (Beneficial for lower back)—Lie on stomach, hands straight by the side, palms touching the rights— raise left leg while inhaling—hold and then lower while exhaling. Repeat with right leg. (5-6 times)

Dhanurasana—Lie flat on stomach, bend legs backwards and hold with hand—rise while inhaling—hold—and down while exhaling (5-6 times)

Tarasana—Stand straight with legs 6-7 inches apart, arm to the side. While inhaling rise on toes while raising arms slowly taking them right up and then joining the fingers above the head palm upward—hold hand then return to initial position while exhaling. Arms to be raised from the front and lowered by the side. (4-5 times)

21

Personality of the New Millennium

The times are changing and so are the needs of the new millennium. There is fierce competition for reaching the top. In any profession you need to be of top quality and put your best foot forward to excel. **Philip Crosby,** the quality guru says, 'The executives of the new business environment will have to be a complete personality, smarter and more thorough with and about dealing with the real world than their 20th century counterpart'.

As suggested by Philip, we may like to list important features for the person who can succeed in the race in the 21st century. The key characteristics, which need to be developed appropriately, that would help present professionals to become tomorrow's leaders are:

1. **Strategic Awareness:** Earlier if you were doing your job honestly, it could comfortably take you to greater

heights. But these days you must be clear with your objective. If the awareness of the strategic route to the final goal is clear you may be the winner at the end of the day.

2. **Adaptability in new structure and work culture:** If you are rigid and not ready to change, you may not be welcome at any important organisation. You may be a genius in your own eyes, but an organisation wants a team player and adaptability to the new work culture and the new structure is desired in almost all the organisations.

3. **Ability to work in International team:** The world is getting closer and distances between countries are getting smaller with the speed of information technology and globalisation of the world economy. If you still like to keep your concept of sticking to your local cult, you will be lagging behind in the race. 'Think global and act local' is the slogan all over the world. We must learn to transform in the global environment.

4. **Language Skills:** Which languages are required to improve your personality may be a very difficult question. But as we can see for ourselves that globalisation and for people to meet the international requirement one needs skilful use of the international language such as English. Be more particular to sharpen your language skills in the new millennium.

5. **Basic understanding of financial viability and its importance:** All the important work you are doing in any sphere of life has to be financially viable. Any

thing great but not economically viable shall be summarily rejected. Therefore you must learn the basic economic lessons. Give a thought about whatever you plan in that perspective in the new millennium.

6. **High task orientation:** As the competition is getting fierce and tough, we may be required to be more task-oriented. You cannot leave anything to chance. Make sure everything you have done is as per the plan.

7. **Human relationship:** For the last few decades the importance of human relationship has come to the fore, but in the new millennium, in the age of knowledge and information, the importance of human relationships will be foremost. The relationships will be the pivotal force for all successful ventures. Therefore if you want to prepare yourself for the new millennium, sharpen your relationship skills.

8. **Self-reliance:** The new millennium has compelled each and every individual to rely on self-confidence and only a person with self-confidence will win the race.

The reasons why a man fails

Napoleon Hill has conducted surveys for different kind of persons in different walks of life. Based on a large sample survey and its analysis, he came up with a very interesting list of thirty reasons for failures, which are valid for any person in any country and at any point of time. I will suggest all readers to go through the list of thirty weaknesses. If you overcome and avoid these you need not worry. In this millennium you may be the most effective person with extraordinary personality if you can cope with the following points:

1. Unfavourable hereditary weakness—this is the only area where no one can help you but certainly you can always choose other works, where your strength lie.
2. Lack of well defined purpose of life.
3. Lack of ambition to aim above mediocrity.
4. Insufficient education.
5. Lack of self-discipline.
6. Ill-health.
7. Unfavourable environmental influence on your childhood.
8. Procrastination.
9. Lack of persistence – good starter but poor finisher.
10. Negative personality – if you repel people mind it.
11. Control on urge for sex.
12. Lack of well defined power of decision.
13. One of major six fears.
14. Wrong selection of mate in marriage.
15. Over caution.
16. Wrong selection of associates in business.
17. Superstition and prejudice.
18. Wrong selection of a vocation.
19. Lack of concentration on efforts.
20. The habit of indiscriminate spending.
21. Lack of enthusiasm.
22. Intolerance.
23. Intemperance.

24. Inability to co-operate with others.
25. Possession of power, which was not acquired by effort.
26. Intentional dishonesty.
27. Egoism.
28. Lack of capital.
29. Guessing instead of thinking.
30. Any other name or cause, which has caused failure for you in particular.

What is the Indian way of a successful personality?

There are many great personalities in India, but the man who did all the hard work to navigate India into the new millennium of information age is Narayan Murthy, a middle class Indian, who must be the example to be followed by any individual who has dreams to fulfil. He says, 'Every dream should be given shape and never bother too much for basic needs such as food, shelter and health. Try for something worthwhile even if it seems impossible. Put the interest of the community above your own. You are not sacrificing anything if you are doing this. In a poor community it is difficult to become rich and happy.' He has given some very basic tips to transform your personality for the new millennium.

Be your own role model

Make yourself, your role model: the best model for any person is he himself. The great Gandhian philosophy is to set yourself as your own example. Start doing your job honestly, work hard and do not complain about the difficulties you face. We do not get so many opportunities, if we get any we must not let them go. Murthy says that we need more engineers, doctors, and chartered accountants, but above all we need people with right attitude.

Compare yourself with the best

Good executive quality needs to be compared with the best, the person should not accept the standard, which exists, but benchmark the best in the world. In this, we must not expect much from the Government. The Government may or may not be in a position to provide good number of jobs or remove poverty. It is up to us to make the system more conducive for our own growth.

Share your dreams with others

Share your dreams with others: we can fulfil the dreams of the team if we can inspire others also for a bigger dream. The great names in the Indian industry such as Kurien, Bhabha, Pitroda and Abdul Kalam are few names that were never bogged down by the circumstances and the limitation of infrastructure.

Mind versus Mindset

Mindset can be the biggest bottleneck. Having good qualities and competence is not sufficient to excel. Having a positive attitude and a right mindset is very critical to achieve success. The numbers told by politicians, bureaucrats and businessmen regarding shortages and resource limitation are only to create a sense of scarcity, coming from a weak mind. Most of the East Asian countries like Singapore and Malaysia a few years back had scarce resources, at least we have the basic infrastructure to make the best use of it. There is a continuous struggle between mind and mindset; those who win the battle of mindset will trigger the process of transformation.

Spend time with young people, it will allow you to think fresh and bold.

The young generation are oozing with energy and have new and innovative ideas. In any organisation which has performed well, the energy of these young people has been channelled in the right direction. The company of young people will never allow you to feel tired.

Case Study I

Mukesh Chopra, 49, is a seasoned Manager of Maruti Industry, a leading firm in the Indian automobile sector. He has been serving the same company for the last twenty-four years. Last year he had been assigned a new responsibility of heading Operations Restructuring Division. The restructuring has changed the perceptions of working of several departments, some of the older record keeping functions are no longer required and the company desired to give it up for the information technology centre, which can take care of all these over heads. He was waiting to see the results of other departments before plunging into action.

Amit Munjal, 35, the Marketing Manager in the same office is a pro-reform person who has proposed to implement the CRM software of SAP (a software package, which provides total solution for specific functional areas). He was the key person to implement the CRM (Customer Relationship Management) and all the dealers and suppliers were also asked to start the B2B (Business to Business) model of CRM implementation. The project was worth thirty crore and was planned for implementation through one of the SAP Consultants. The project was aimed to reduce the inventory level drastically and help to implement the JIT (Just in Time) concept for the unit. If successfully implemented the project can break even in three years time.

The project was implemented on time and the first six months proved a learning period for the employees as well as the dealers and suppliers. The persons started using it once they could overcome the initial inhibitions. The returns of the investment in the first financial year were marginally on the negative side.

The company President was taking an annual appraisal for all the senior executives in the company. As he was reviewing the IT implementation, Chopra was very vocal against the IT projects and said that it had done no good to the company and established norms were more comfortable as compared to the new system. He quoted the example of huge CRM expenditure in the marketing department, which had not proved very fruitful. He said to the President, 'Over the last one year, most of my ambitious colleagues have undertaken very expensive IT projects. But I am sorry to inform that they have failed.'

'I have not taken undue risk but have found it more useful to wait and watch to see the results in other departments.'

The President said, 'I am ready to lose a few of my hard earned rupees on such ambitious projects rather than drinking coffee and only discussing the outcome.'

Questions:

1. Which approach is economically beneficial to the company?
2. Is Mukesh Chopra's attitude the right attitude?
3. If you are in the CEO's chair what will be your next move?

22

Pray to God for Your Well-being

I am not discussing anything religious pertaining to any particular religion or sect. There may be some debate on whether or not the help of God can help us achieve strength in our personality to face difficult periods in life. But one thing is for sure that we shall be deprived of any such benefit if we cannot seek help from Him during distress. You are not going to loose a single penny if you pray to God.

God is everywhere. He blesses us all the time. There may be doubts in our mind that if this is true then why some of the calls remain unanswered? Why is there discrimination by God, some are rich, some are poor and others are weak and some are strong? Some get more of God's grace whereas others do not get it at all.

| GOD | → | Your Mind | → | YOU |

The arrow shows the blessings of God flowing to a person. It is always there for everyone. But before it reaches one, it meets one's mind. Only if the mind is calm and free from bad and evil thoughts, the blessing will reach you. If the mind is full of anger, fear and other bad thoughts, they block God's blessing from reaching the person.

There is this big question of how to keep the mind calm and happy? We can find out the ways and means of keeping ourself cool and calm at the time of distress. Some of the easy ways are:

1. **Allow only happy thoughts:** Think only about happy thoughts: we all go through several situations and experiences throughout the day, some are good, some may be not so good. It is up to us, which thought we take as our legacy and try to live with. There are some people who always quote the bad and painful days of their life. Recently I was travelling on an official assignment with a senior executive of an MNC. Throughout the one hour journey he explained to me the bad times the previous year due to illness that he suffered. I enquired if he is all right now. He said of course yes! But he prefers to live with his sorrow. Whereas there are some people, who always remember their youthful college days that keep them young at heart forever.

2. **See, hear and talk about good things:** It is our choice whether we are interested to see the good side of the world or the bad side. Some of the advisors in your

colleges may advise that life is not complete if you have not experienced some of the so-called unaccepted practices in the society. Mind it, you never need to experience any bad things to understand whether it is bad for you and society. Do you need to drink poison to see how it affects you? Bad things can never ever have a good effect. Have you seen any drunkard praying to God after consuming liquor?

3. **Help others to come out from bad habits:** We all live for our own self. But a person who spends some of his time, energy and part of his income on others, particularly those who are needy and not so privileged, are more satisfied. The satisfaction and peace of mind it gives will be much more valuable than any other thing.

4. **Pray a while each day:** Prayers will give you the confidence to face the world. The benefits of praying are not restricted to a place of worship but any place on earth. The greatest author in modern times, Norman Vincent Peale has put it very correctly, *'Every problem can be solved and solved rightly if you pray. Affirmative prayer releases Power by which positive results are accomplished.'* He has recommended very basic ten steps to pray to God every day:

- Set aside a few minutes everyday, even if you do not have anything to pray, just keep remembering God.
- Try to speak orally a few words to God, in your own language, simple, natural words.

- If you are very busy, pray when you are going for your daily routine to office or college in a bus, taxi, train or an elevator.
- Never pray to ask something from God, use it to thank Him for everything.
- God can protect you from all evils, have faith in him and reassure yourself by saying words of praise.
- Never use a negative thought in a prayer, the results can be obtained only if you have positive thinking.
- God always gives better than what you ask for, always express your willingness to accept God's will.
- Same as what the great epic Bhagwad Gita conveys us, Vincent also suggests we must do our duty and leave the results in the hands of God.
- Even pray for the people who have not treated you well, this will help you to improve relationships and forgive others for their mistakes.

References

1. Dale Carnegie, 'How to Win Friends and Influence People' Vermillion Publication, 1953.
2. Napolean Hill, 'Think and Grow Rich' Master Mind Books, India with N H Foundation, 1966.
3. Norman Vincent Peale, 'The Power of Positive Thinking' Vermillion Publication, 1953.
4. Steven Covey, 'Seven Habits of Highly Effective People' Simon and Schuster, London, 1989.
5. Shiva Khera, 'You can Win' Macmillan Publisher, 1998.
6. Arindam Chaudhri, 'Count the Chickens Before they Hatch', Vikas Publishers Pvt. Ltd., 2000.
7. Morgan, King and Robinson, 'Introduction to Psychology' Tata Mcgraw Hill, 1998.
8. Ahiya K.K., 'Organisational Behaviour' Kalyani Publishers, New Delhi, 1990.
9. Harris Thomas, 'I am O.K. and You are O.K.' Arrow, 1995.
10. Hall and Lindzey, 'Theories of Personalities' Willey Eastern, New Delhi, 1978.

11. Joginder Singh, 'Success and Happiness' Alka Publishers, New Delhi, 1998.
12. S.N. Chary, 'Business Guru Speak' Macmillan India Limited, 2001.
13. Radhika Krishnakumar, 'Garden of Life' Macmillan India Limited, 1996.

The last but certainly not the least, for developing a great personality, which you are, I am telling you the last step. Follow these simple ideologies in letter and spirit. If you can apply the six sentences in your routine, you must have understood the crux of the book.

A short course in human relationship:

The six most important words are: 'I admit I made a mistake.'
The five most important words are: 'You did a good job.'
The four most important words are: 'What is your opinion?'
The three most important words are: 'If you please.'
The two most important words are: 'Thank you.'
The least important word is: 'I'.

Exercise-II

Firo-B – is the common name of an interesting and very common tool used by many of the behavioural scientists to find out what is the behaviour of a person towards other group members in his team or society in general. The Firo-B technique will determine the expressed and wanted behaviour in respect of inclusion (social behaviour), control (exercising command) and affection (love). You are required to plot it on a Matrix, based on the scores in the questionnaire in the next page. The expressed behaviour will tell about the behaviour people express towards their team members and how they expect others to behave. You are required to answer all the questions in the answer sheet with honest assertion and once you have answered them you may fill the form as annexure. You need to add the answer of the question which is right in each block, and then sum it up. After completing this exercise you are required to read the paragraph written below for your own analysis. You may also take help of a friend to analyse it more effectively.

If you have scored more than seven in any block you are an extreme behaving person on higher side, similarly if you have scored less than three, that indicates you have a tendency to be extreme on the lower side. Most persons fall in the moderate range and their behaviour towards others are in the scale of 3-7. If there are two persons with complementary desired and wanted behaviour they will be a perfect match for each other.

Few of the analyses for extreme behavioural traits can be as below:

EI – 9, this person will be an extrovert and would like all others to be part of his activities.
EI – 0, is an introvert.
WI – 9, extremely social.
WI – 0, lonely and aloof.
EC – 9, highly controlled all the time, high responsibility level.
EC – 9, low responsibilities, does not want to be accountable for any thing.
WC – 9, highly submissive, dependent on others.
WC – 0, he is a rebel and does not want to be guided by set rules.
EA – 9, every one should love and like him, desire need is very high.
EA – 0, they are not bothered, no one likes him. He is afraid others may not like him. He has negative thoughts in his mind.

The expressed and wanted must match and complement for the spouses otherwise there is a chance of conflict in the relationship.

GROUP _____
DATE _____
MALE ___ FEMALE ___
AGE ___

NAME _____

FIRO-B

	I	C
e		
w		

Please place the number of the answer that best applies to you in the box at the left of the statement.
Please be as honest as you can

☐ 1. I try to be with people
    1. usually 2. often 3. sometimes 4. occasionally 5. rarely 6. never

☐ 2. I let other people decide what to do
    1. usually 2. often 3. sometimes 4. occasionally 5. rarely 6. never

☐ 3. I join social groups
    1. usually 2. often 3. sometimes 4. occasionally 5. rarely 6. never

☐ 4. I try to have close relationships with people
    1. usually 2. often 3. sometimes 4. occasionally 5. rarely 6. never

☐ 5. I tend to join social organisations when I have an opportunity.
    1. usually 2. often 3. sometimes 4. occasionally 5. rarely 6. never

☐ 6. I let other people strongly influence my actions
    1. usually 2. often 3. sometimes 4. occasionally 5. rarely 6. never

☐ 7. I try to be included in informal social activities.
    1. usually 2. often 3. sometimes 4. occasionally 5. rarely 6. never

8. I try to have close, personal relationships with people
   1. usually 2. often 3. sometimes 4. occasionally 5. rarely 6. never
9. I try to include other people in my plans
   1. usually 2. often 3. sometimes 4. occasionally 5. rarely 6. never
10. I let other people control my actions
    1. usually 2. often 3. sometimes 4. occasionally 5. rarely 6. never
11. I try to have people around me
    1. usually 2. often 3. sometimes 4. occasionally 5. rarely 6. never
12. I try to get close and personal with people
    1. usually 2. often 3. sometimes 4. occasionally 5. rarely 6. never
13. When people are doing things together I tend to join them
    1. usually 2. often 3. sometimes 4. occasionally 5. rarely 6. never
14. I am easily led by people
    1. usually 2. often 3. sometimes 4. occasionally 5. rarely 6. never
15. I try to avoid being alone
    1. usually 2. often 3. sometimes 4. occasionally 5. rarely 6. never
16. I try to participate in group activities
    1. usually 2. often 3. sometimes 4. occasionally 5. rarely 6. never
17. I try to be friendly to people
    1. most people 2. many people 3. some people 4. a few people 5. one/two people 6. nobody
18. I let other people decide what to do
    1. most people 2. many people 3. some people 4. a few people 5. one or two people 6. nobody

19. My personal relations with people are cool and distant
    1. most people   2. many people   3. some people   4. a few people   5. one or two people   6. nobody

20. I let other people take charge of things
    1. most people   2. many people   3. some people   4. a few people   5. one or two people   6. nobody

21. I try to have close relationships with people
    1. most people   2. many people   3. some people   4. a few people   5. one or two people   6. nobody

22. I let other people strongly influence my actions
    1. most people   2. many people   3. some people   4. a few people   5. one or two people   6. nobody

23. I try to get close and personal with people
    1. most people   2. many people   3. some people   4. a few people   5. one or two people   6. nobody

24. I let other people control my actions
    1. most people   2. many people   3. some people   4. a few people   5. one or two people   6. nobody

25. I act cool and distant with people
    1. most people   2. many people   3. some people   4. a few people   5. one or two people   6. nobody

26. I am easily led by people
    1. most people   2. many people   3. some people   4. a few people   5. one or two people   6. nobody

27. I try to have close personal relationships with people
   1. most people   2. many people   3. some people   4. a few people   5. one or two people   6. nobody

28. I like people to invite me to things
   1. most people   2. many people   3. some people   4. a few people   5. one or two people   6. nobody

29. I like people to get close and personal with me
   1. most people   2. many people   3. some people   4. a few people   5. one or two people   6. nobody

30. I try to influence strongly other people's actions
   1. most people   2. many people   3. some people   4. a few people   5. one or two people   6. nobody

31. I like people to invite me to join in their activities
   1. most people   2. many people   3. some people   4. a few people   5. one or two people   6. nobody

32. I like people to act close toward me
   1. most people   2. many people   3. some people   4. a few people   5. one or two people   6. nobody

33. I try to take charge of things when I am with people
   1. most people   2. many people   3. some people   4. a few people   5. one or two people   6. nobody

34. I like people to include me in their activities
   1. most people   2. many people   3. some people   4. a few people   5. one or two people   6. nobody

35. I like people to act cool and distant toward me
    1. most people 2. many people 3. some people 4. a few people 5. one or two people 6. nobody

36. I try to have other people do things the way I want them done
    1. most people 2. many people 3. some people 4. a few people 5. one or two people 6. nobody

37. I like people to ask me to participate in their discussions
    1. most people 2. many people 3. some people 4. a few people 5. one or two people 6. nobody

38. I like people to act friendly toward me
    1. most people 2. many people 3. some people 4. a few people 5. one or two people 6. nobody

39. I like people to invite me to participate in their activities
    1. most people 2. many people 3. some people 4. a few people 5. one or two people 6. nobody

40. I like people to act distant toward me
    1. most people 2. many people 3. some people 4. a few people 5. one or two people 6. nobody

41. I try to be the dominant person when I am with people
    1. usually 2. often 3. sometimes 4. occasionally 5. rarely 6. never

42. I like people to invite me to things
    1. usually 2. often 3. sometimes 4. occasionally 5. rarely 6. never

43. I like people to act close toward me
    1. usually 2. often 3. sometimes 4. occasionally 5. rarely 6. never

44. I try to have other people do things I want done
    1. usually 2. often 3. sometimes 4. occasionally 5. rarely 6. never

- [ ] 45. I like people to invite me to join their activities
        1. usually   2. often   3. sometimes   4. occasionally   5. rarely   6. never
- [ ] 46. I like people to act cool and distant towards me
        1. usually   2. often   3. sometimes   4. occasionally   5. rarely   6. never
- [ ] 47. I try to influence strongly other people's actions
        1. usually   2. often   3. sometimes   4. occasionally   5. rarely   6. never
- [ ] 48. I like people to include me in their activities
        1. usually   2. often   3. sometimes   4. occasionally   5. rarely   6. never
- [ ] 49. I like people to act close and personal with me
        1. usually   2. often   3. sometimes   4. occasionally   5. rarely   6. never
- [ ] 50. I try to take charge of things when I'm with people
        1. usually   2. often   3. sometimes   4. occasionally   5. rarely   6. never
- [ ] 51. I like people to invite me to participate in their activities
        1. usually   2. often   3. sometimes   4. occasionally   5. rarely   6. never
- [ ] 52. I like people to act distant toward me
        1. usually   2. often   3. sometimes   4. occasionally   5. rarely   6. never
- [ ] 53. I try to have other people do things the way I want them done
        1. usually   2. often   3. sometimes   4. occasionally   5. rarely   6. never
- [ ] 54. I take charge of things when I'm with people
        1. usually   2. often   3. sometimes   4. occasionally   5. rarely   6. never

FIRO-B

SCORING SHEET

	INCLUSION		CONTROL		AFFECTION	
EXPRESSED TOWARDS OTHERS	1	1 – 2 – 3	30	1 – 2 – 3	4	1 – 2
	3	1 – 2 – 3 –,4	33	1 – 2 – 3	8	1 – 2
	5	1 – 2 – 3	36	1 – 2	12	1
	7	1 – 2 – 3 – 4	41	1 – 2 – 3 – 4	17	1 – 2
	9	1 – 2	44	1 – 2 – 3	19	4 – 5 – 6
	11	1 – 2	47	1 – 2 – 3	21	1 – 2
	13	1 – 2	50	1 – 2	23	1 – 2
	15	1	53	1 – 2	25	1 – 2
	16	1	54	1 – 2	27	1 – 2
	Total		Total		Total	
WANTED FROM OTHERS	28	1 – 2	2	1 – 2 – 3 – 4	29	1 – 2
	31	1 – 2	6	1 – 2 – 3 – 4	32	1 – 2
	34	1 – 2	10	1 – 2 – 3	35	5 – 6
	37	1	14	1 – 2 – 3	38	1 – 2
	39	1	18	1 – 2 – 3 – 4	40	5 – 6
	42	1 – 2	20	1 – 2 – 3 – 4	43	1
	45	1 – 2	22	1 – 2 – 3 – 4	46	5 – 6
	48	1 – 2	24	1 – 2 – 3	49	1 – 2
	51	1 – 2	26	1 – 2	52	5 – 6
	Total		Total		Total	